New Island / New Drama   **Series Editor** / Dermot Bolger

GREATEST HITS

Four Irish One-Act Plays

Blood Guilty   Antoine Ó Flatharta

The Marlboro Man   Clare Dowling

Greatest Hits   Thomas McLaughlin

Faint Voices   John MacKenna

GREATEST HITS

Four Irish One-Act Plays

Blood Guilty   Antoine Ó Flatharta

The Marlboro Man   Clare Dowling

Greatest Hits   Thomas McLaughlin

Faint Voices   John MacKenna

Edited by Dermot Bolger

DUBLIN

GREATEST HITS
Four Irish One-Act Plays
is first published in 1997
in Ireland by
New Island Books,
2 Brookside,
Dundrum Road,
Dublin 14,
Ireland
& in Britain by
Nick Hern Books
14 Larden Road,
London W3 7ST.

All plays copyright to their individual authors.
Copyright © 1997.

ISBN 1 874597 61 8 (New Island Books)
ISBN 1 85459 352 8 (Nick Hern Books)

New Island Books receives financial assistance from
The Arts Council (An Chomhairle Ealaíon), Dublin,
Ireland.

Top cover photo by Fergus Bourke of Stuart Dunne as John
and Kevin Flood as Dan in *Blood Guilty.* Lower cover photo
by Nick Heagney of Conor Mullen as Mick and Donna Dent as
Wanda in *The Marlboro Man.*
Cover design by Jon Berkeley
Typeset by Graphic Resources
Printed in Ireland by Colour Books, Ltd.

Contents

Blood Guilty   11

The Marlboro Man   41

Greatest Hits   69

Faint Voices   103

BLOOD GUILTY

A One-Act Play

Antoine Ó Flatharta

Blood Guilty was first performed at the **Peacock Theatre,** Dublin on Thursday 17th August 1989 with the following cast:

PAT	John Cowley
DAN	Kevin Flood
JOHN	Stuart Dunne
TOM	Jim Bruton
Design	Jan Bee Brown
Lighting	Mick Doyle
Director	Caroline FitzGerald

TIME

The Late 1980s

LOCATION

Rural Ireland

We remain human only by changing.
Each generation must create its own humanity.

— Edward Bond

BLOOD GUILTY

Before the light goes up we hear the sound of a French radio station broadcasting a news programme on long wave.

The light comes up. The set could be the "Abbey kitchen" of the 1950s, were it not for the fact that there are some plastic bags, milk cartons, etc. around to show we are in the late 1980s.

DAN, a blind man in his late sixties, sits in a chair upstage. By his side is a transistor radio broadcasting a news programme in French. PAT, his brother, who is in his seventies, sits nearby reading a Sunday newspaper. He speaks to DAN without looking up from his paper.

PAT: Turn it down or turn it over. *(DAN pays no attention. Finally, PAT looks up from his paper.)*

PAT: Turn it down or turn it over I said. *(Again, DAN pays him no attention but continues to listen to the radio with his eyes closed. PAT suddenly gets up and turns off the radio. He goes back to his chair and sits down. As soon as he does, DAN switches the radio back on. PAT throws down his paper.)*

PAT: No! No! No! You'll drive me mad. Why are you doin' it to me? Why?

DAN: It's my only company. I found it.

PAT: You found it? What kind of talk is that?

DAN: It's coming from miles away.

PAT: And you don't know a word of it! Why won't you listen to something you can understand then you mad old goat? That's a foreign station you're listening to.

DAN: I know.

PAT: You don't know a word of what they're sayin'. It's gettin' madder you are. Gettin' madder by the bloody day. I could have you put away any time I want. The doctor said I only have to sign the form. Remember that.

(DAN pays him no attention but continues to listen to the foreign station. PAT looks at him and shakes his head. He gets up and turns off the radio again.)

PAT: Anything could be happening. They could be exploding the atom bomb and we wouldn't know a thing about it.

DAN: It would be on the foreign station.

PAT: *(Getting angry.)* It would! It would, but what good would that be to us! We wouldn't know what they're sayin'!

DAN: We'd know.

PAT: How would we know? We don't have a word of the language...why am I wastin' my breath on you. Do you know what I was readin' in that paper? I was readin' about a man over in England who took a shotgun and went out and shot everyone he met. Even his mother. Then he shot himself. I think I know what was in that man's mind. *(Pause)* I'm banning the foreign station. Are you listening to me? If I see you going near that knob again I'm signing the form.

(DAN closes his eyes and doesn't reply. PAT looks at him. It's clear he is already sorry and starting to feel guilty. It's also clear that it's an endless cat-and-mouse the two brothers have been playing for many years. Lately, the arguments have become more frequent and direct. PAT sits down and takes up the paper again. He looks at the story he is reading.)

PAT: It's a terrible story...he just lost his mind...do you want me to read it to you?

(DAN doesn't reply.)

PAT: You can put the radio on if you leave off the foreign station. That's just wastin' the batteries. And drivin' me into the ground with it...will I put a right station on for you? *(PAT* *gets up and turns on the radio, tuning it till he finds an Irish talk station.)* Now. Listen to that and don't be like a madman. *(PAT goes back to reading his paper. As soon as he has settled down, DAN takes the radio and retunes it to the French station. PAT gets up angrily and confronts his brother.)*

PAT: Why are you doin' this to me? Answer me that question? Answer me that question will you? If it wasn't for you I wouldn't be here. I could be anywhere...over in Montana... anywhere. "A year from today I'll be over in Montana." That's what I used to say when I was younger.

(DAN increases the radio volume. PAT angrily switches it off.)

PAT: I could murder you. Often, I could murder you. I could bury you alive and not care twopence.

(DAN puts out his hand to turn on the radio. PAT catches his arm, as if he is about to strike him. He stops.)

PAT: I'll have to put you away. I'll have to, because if I don't, if I don't...some night I'll take the tongs and split your head open. I'll bury you out in the garden and no one will be the wiser.

(DAN puts out his hand again and turns the radio on. Again, we hear the French station. PAT stands in front of him. Finally he speaks.)

PAT: We're driving each other mad. Tomorrow morning, tomorrow morning I'm signing that form. I'm calling the doctor and signing that form. I should have done it years ago. Years ago. *(PAT goes over to a side table and picks up a pair of binoculars lying there. He holds it.)* Not a sinner for miles. God's curse on whatever it was brought us onto this earth. *(He puts down the binoculars.)* I could be over in America. Could be as good as the next one. *(He looks over at PAT.)* Families are the curse of God.

(PAT stands there looking at his brother, the French station still on. Finally he walks to the door, takes his jacket and goes out. As soon as PAT leaves, DAN increases the radio volume. He relaxes in his chair. He could be sleeping, but he isn't. He is listening to the foreign station. The image should be held

for a time, the stillness, the strangeness. The mood is broken by a loud knock at the door. DAN leans forward in his chair and turns down the radio volume. The knock is repeated. DAN slowly gets to his feet and makes his way to the door. He opens it. JOHN and TOM are standing there. TOM is holding the blankets.)

DAN: Yes?

JOHN: Would you be interested in buying some blankets?

DAN: Blankets?

TOM: Yeah. Pure wool. Best quality. We only have a few left, everyone's buyin' them...it's going to be a cold winter...you won't find a better bargain...you're welcome to have a look at them.

JOHN: Look, it's freezing out here, mind if we come in. *(They enter.)*

JOHN: Is there someone else in the house with you?

DAN: No. *(They move around, showing their disgust at what is to them squalid conditions.)*

JOHN: *(To TOM)* Put them down.

(TOM puts the blankets down on the floor. The French station is still playing.)

TOM: *(To DAN)* Are you a foreigner?

JOHN: Don't be an eejit.

TOM: *(To DAN)* You're learning a language.

DAN: I'm a blind man. I can't see what you're selling.

JOHN: Well, we'll give you our word. Our word is our bond. They're top quality blankets, real wool.

TOM: We wouldn't con a blind man.

JOHN: Come on over here, sit down and I'll show you.

(JOHN takes DAN's arm, starts to show him a chair — the wrong one. DAN stiffens. This is the first time anyone has touched him in many years.)

JOHN: Okay, okay. Sit where you like.

(DAN goes and sits in his chair.)

TOM: Want to hear how we got them? They were smuggled across the border. A shop was bombed, you see...

DAN: What kind of shop?

JOHN: A blanket shop.

DAN: They bombed a blanket shop?

JOHN: Yeah. Animals, aren't they? Anyway, they fell into our hands and we're selling them for half-nothing.

DAN: Did this bomb kill people?

JOHN: What?

TOM: No...no...no one was killed...they gave a warning.

DAN: Is there blood on the blankets?

JOHN: Jesus!

TOM: Look, we didn't get them from the North. That's only a story we tell people to make them think they're getting a bargain...

JOHN: Which they are.

TOM: We buy them wholesale. Up in Dublin. Wool mixture. Better than wool, last longer. Fire resistant too. *(JOHN takes the plastic wrapping off one of the blankets. He hands it to DAN.)*

JOHN: Feel the quality. See how heavy it is.

(DAN switches off the radio. JOHN takes another blanket and pushes it into DAN's hands.)

JOHN: Weighs a ton. They'd keep out the frost.

TOM: (*Quietly to JOHN*) We should go, John.

JOHN: Shut up.

DAN: You're brothers, aren't you?

TOM: How'd you know that? (*DAN smiles.*)

JOHN: From our voices, you fool. (*To DAN*) Are you buyin'?

TOM: It's a lovely blanket mister. Full a colours. An' big stripes. Orange, blue, yellow, green. (*DAN is now holding a blanket in his hands. It is multicoloured like an Indian rug. He shifts it from hand to hand.*)

JOHN: A tenner. It's for nothing.

DAN: I only have twenties.

TOM: We'll give you three for twenty.

JOHN: He's going t'ruin me business one a these days.

TOM: Do you mind me asking you, how can you tell the difference between the notes?

JOHN: Are you sure there isn't anyone else living here with you?

DAN: Not a soul. (*JOHN sees the binoculars.*)

JOHN: What's a blind man doin' with a pair of binoculars I wonder?

TOM: Million years old. But I'd say they're good ones.

JOHN: (*To TOM*) Put them down.

TOM: And women's shoes. Shoes! Pair of women's shoes over here, John! (*To DAN*) You go in for a bit of dressin' up do ya?

JOHN: What was the last time ya cleaned this place?

TOM: Yeah, things breed in dust like this ya know. (*TOM is now over by the table.*) Shouldn't leave the sliced loaf out like that for the flies. (*Picks up cheese carton.*) Galtee cheese. You like peas, too, don't you? Mountain a tins outside your door. Why don't you grow your own things? Livin' out this far...

JOHN: We could rob you.

TOM: Don't mind him.

JOHN: We could murder you and no one would know.

(TOM looks at JOHN. It is as if he has heard this line before. He looks away.)

DAN: How would you murder me?

JOHN: I could stab you.

DAN: You could bury me alive.

(JOHN looks at him. TOM starts to gather up the blankets.)

TOM: Leave him. Can't you see he's crazy.

JOHN: Give us all the money you have in the house and we won't lay a finger on you. Plus we'll leave you a free blanket. Couldn't be fairer.

(TOM is looking at JOHN, aware of how quickly the mood has changed and how easily they have slid into this.)

DAN: Who are you?

TOM: We'll go, John.

JOHN: We've come a long way to visit you in your shit-coloured bog hole. You could be a bit more welcoming.

TOM: *(To JOHN)* Come on, let's go.

JOHN: A lot of old people have been murdered in lonely places like this this winter. Know that?

DAN: Was it you that murdered them?

JOHN: Yeah. Some of them.

(TOM puts the blankets down. He sits on the edge of the table and lights a cigarette. There is suddenly a change of atmosphere. A real sense of danger in the air. It is as if by placing down the

blankets and deciding to stay a tragedy has been set in motion. We don't know, and in a way it doesn't matter, if JOHN is telling the truth. The young men may or may not be murderers. Things are now happening moment to moment.)

JOHN: We only want the money. Every penny you have in the house. You can live.

DAN: And I get a free blanket.

TOM: You can have the lot. I'm not carrying them any further.

JOHN: Shut up you.

TOM: Sick a this crack.

JOHN: So what d'ya say Mr Blind Man with the binoculars?

(DAN sits down on his chair by the radio. He turns on the French station and throws a blanket towards JOHN.)

DAN: I say you can keep your blankets. More weight in an old sack.

(The blanket hits JOHN in the face. A speck of dust gets into his eye.)

JOHN: *(Rubbing his eye.)* You old fucker.

TOM: Some look in his eyes when he did that John! Like Freddy back from the grave!

JOHN: *(To TOM)* Have a look around. *(TOM sighs and gets up.)*

TOM: I mean it. I'm leaving them here. I've carried them far enough.

JOHN: Shut up and look. So me blankets aren't heavy enough for you bogman.

(TOM starts to rummage around in old jars, jugs and cardboard boxes. He finds nothing except lots of old government forms and notices, old almanacs, old calendars and old yellowing rate payment slips. He empties the stuff out on the floor.)

TOM: Why are you keeping all the old calendars?

JOHN: Suppose we should have heavy-duty blankets just for you. Bogman's special.

TOM: *(Looks at calendar.)* 1950. Jesus. There's stuff here going back to day one. *(He takes an old yellowing postcard. Reads it.)* "The vet will be in your area at 11 a.m. next Friday...August 11th 1961." *(He looks over at DAN.)* Did he come?

DAN: He did.

JOHN: Stop messin' you and look for the money.

(TOM finds a stack of old magazines.)

TOM: "Old Hoor's Almanac," oh sorry, "Old Moore's Almanac 1964." Must have kept every scrap of paper that ever came into the house.

JOHN: Are ya goin to tell us where the famous twenties are Freddy?

(JOHN goes and stands in front of DAN. He is holding a blanket. TOM now finds an old booklet, "Bás Beatha", sent out by the government in the mid-1960s to tell people what to do if a nuclear war breaks out.)

TOM: Look at this... "what to do if a nuclear war is declared. Always have the radio by your side...always have a spare set of batteries in the house..."

JOHN: Shut the fuck up and find the money!

(TOM looks at the booklet, shakes his head and throws it on the floor on top of the other pile of stuff.)

TOM: You have a strange collection here old man.

JOHN: *(In front of DAN)* Tell us where the money is.

TOM: The old fool could be skint.

JOHN: He has the money. Haven't you?

DAN: Yes.

JOHN: Where is it?

(JOHN moves in towards DAN and places the blanket over his head. He holds it down.)

JOHN: Where is it?

(TOM is still searching. The French programme is still on the radio. After a few seconds JOHN takes the blanket away from DAN's face. The old man gasps for breath. TOM looks over and starts to search with more vigour.)

JOHN: I'm giving you one more chance. Next time I put this blanket over your head, you're dead.

(TOM finds an old faded photograph. A man and a woman, standing stiff and frozen, dressed up to the nines in a turn-of-the-century photographic studio.)

TOM: I found his father and mother.

JOHN: Keep your fuckin' mind on what you're doing!

TOM: *(Reads back of photo.)* "Hall's Studio. Boston. 1902." *(JOHN looks over at TOM.)*

JOHN: For fuck's sake...

TOM: The shoes! The shoes must have been...

JOHN: I told ya to keep lookin'!

(TOM puts down the photo and continues to search. John moves closer to DAN.)

JOHN: Maybe ya want me to do it Freddy. D'ya know what I'm goin t'tell ya? I think we should be paid money by the government to do jobs like this. We could finish ya off in style. Pictures of yer bog hole on the nine o'clock news. *(He holds the blanket over his head.)* Imagine that, Freddy. For three minutes tomorrow night everyone in the country will be thinkin about ya! *(Tightens blanket.)* Where are yer twenties bogman?

TOM: Look at the way he's wigglin'.

JOHN: Knows he's goin' to be a famous man.

TOM: Say he was a strong bastard in his time.

JOHN: Brutal murder of blind bogman. Then again maybe they'll never find yer body. Someone'll dig ya outa the bog a thousand years from now.

(He holds down the blanket over the old man's head. Suddenly, someone is heard coming to the door. TOM stops searching. JOHN drags DAN from the chair, blanket still over his head. He falls on the floor. TOM goes and stands behind the door.)

JOHN: Who is it? I thought you said you lived alone you old fucker.

TOM: Maybe it's the social worker or someone...

(The door opens and PAT enters.)

PAT: You're the murderers, aren't you?

JOHN: Yeah. We are.

TOM: We only want the money.

PAT: There's no money here.

(JOHN moves forward.)

JOHN: He said there is.

(PAT looks at DAN who is trying to get up from the floor. He goes over to him and helps him into a chair.)

PAT: Have ya killed him?

JOHN: Not yet.

TOM: We're busy people you know, can't do everything.

PAT: *(To DAN)* Did you let them in?

DAN: They're brothers too.

PAT: You let them in. You opened the door and let murderers into the house. After everything I told you. After all the stories.

JOHN: Stop talkin'!

21

(PAT continues to give out to DAN.)

PAT: Told you about the pictures in the Sunday paper. I told you about that man.

(JOHN empties out the contents of an old jug, coins, medals, papers.)

JOHN: We'll take this fuckin bog hole apart!

PAT: Not a mile from here and half his head gone. *(He looks at JOHN and TOM.)* Savages.

TOM: Just give us the money.

PAT: Told you about that woman.

(JOHN goes over to PAT and attempts to push him into a chair.)

JOHN: Sit down you fucker.

PAT: Blood on her face, her sister dead.

TOM: Just say where it is.

(As PAT speaks, he is eyeing a knife on a nearby table. As he moves to get the knife, JOHN jumps and grabs it. He stands in front of PAT, holding the knife.)

JOHN: No way José. You'd like to stick it in my back wouldn't you?

PAT: That sort of death would be too easy for you. I seen pictures of what you done.

TOM: Just give us the money and we'll go.

PAT: You came here to kill us. I knew you'd find us.

(PAT is now standing in front of JOHN, staring straight into his eyes.)

PAT: Kill me and I'll be on your back till the day you die. I'll stick to you like a barnacle. I'll be inside your dirty head like a fat rat. And it won't only be me. It'll be everyone who was murdered round here since Cain killed Abel.

TOM: He's a madman, John.

JOHN: People talk like that when they want to live.

PAT: Did you ever kill a pig? I killed pigs. Killing you now, killing you would be like killing a pig.

TOM: Look at his fuckin' eyes.

JOHN: Come on mister, make my day.

PAT: A few screams, then the eyes would see no more and that would be the end of it. Bacon.

JOHN: Stop answerin' back you fucker.

PAT: Make puddin' outa the blood.

TOM: Jesus it's like *Cannibal County,* remember the video?

JOHN: Keep lookin' you and shut up!

PAT: Kill me, kill me and you'll know what it's like to kill. I'll not go easy.

TOM: *(To JOHN)* Let's go...

JOHN: No. *(JOHN is staring back at PAT, taken aback by the old man's outburst. Finally, he speaks.)* Think that scares me? Think that crap scares me? Think that crap will save your life?

(JOHN quickly pulls the knife and grazes the old man's hand.)

JOHN: See. I don't feel anything inside my dirty head. Bet you feel something though.

(DAN finally gets to his feet. He goes to his chair and sits down. TOM begins to search again for the money.)

TOM: Just tell us where the money is...tell us and nothing will happen.

(PAT is holding the side of his wounded hand in his palm. He looks at the blood. He takes a dirty old handkerchief from his pocket and wraps it around his wound. TOM looks over.)

TOM: Cover it with something clean for fuck's sake. You'll get an infection from that old rag.

PAT: I got an infection the day you were born.

JOHN: Jesus if I had to live here. I'd hang myself if I had to live like you.

PAT: There's a tree outside the window. Will I get you a rope?

JOHN: Don't answer me back you old fucker. Your life is in my hands. *(TOM stops searching.)*

TOM: I give up.

JOHN: Keep lookin'!

TOM: Freddy was goin' to tell us when Rambo came in.

(JOHN takes the blanket and goes over to DAN. He places it over his head once more.)

JOHN: Tell us where it is or he's dead.

PAT: I'd prefer to be buried alive than hand you anything of mine.

(JOHN loosens his grip on the blanket. Suddenly DAN lets out a piercing scream that shocks everyone in the room. JOHN lets the knife fall to the ground. PAT grabs it. He quickly makes a run for JOHN. JOHN steps aside, and TOM who is standing behind him gets stabbed in the side.)

TOM: Jesus Christ...

(JOHN makes a dive for PAT, but the old man holds the knife in front of his face and he quickly backs off. TOM is now on the floor holding his bleeding side.)

TOM: We didn't come here to murder.

(JOHN goes over to his brother.)

JOHN: Are you alright?

TOM: What do you think.

JOHN: Why didn't you step aside...you're fuckin' useless.

(PAT is now standing upstage, holding the bloodied knife in his hand.)

PAT: It isn't a half-starved child who doesn't know who he is or where he is that is going to kill us off.

DAN: Do you have the knife now?

PAT: I do.

TOM: Christ, we have to get out of here John. Look at the blood...just look at all the blood.

(JOHN takes a blanket and puts it around TOM)

DAN: Tell me what's happening.

JOHN: He stabbed my brother.

TOM: We didn't come here to murder.

PAT: Do you deny it then?

TOM: We were just tired.

PAT: Deny it!

TOM: Just tired.

PAT: Murderers.

(DAN quickly turns on the radio. Again, the French station. PAT viciously turns it off again.)

PAT: *(To DAN)* I said I don't want that! Never parade your madness in front of my naked eyes again! Go to bed! Go to bed you. Only for me you'd be dead under a blanket now. *(PAT takes a blanket and looks at it. He reads the label.)* Made in Taiwan. Warm wash 30. Made in Taiwan.

TOM: I think I'm dying.

JOHN: You are not.

PAT: You are. Too true you're dying.

TOM: Give me a drink of water.

(JOHN gets up to get water. PAT comes over and stops him.)

PAT: No water. Did you give them water?

(JOHN takes a small plastic statue that is on the floor nearby. He unscrews the top and holds it to TOM's lips. TOM drinks, then spits it out.)

TOM: It's salty!

JOHN: Drink it.

(TOM looks up into his brother's eyes.)

TOM: I'm dyin', John. I really think I'm dyin'. I'm feeling awful weak and everything...like people say you feel when you're dying...

PAT: Never forget that woman's face.

(JOHN looks over towards PAT.)

JOHN: Let us go and you'll never see us again. I promise.

PAT: Her eye clean taken out of her head.

JOHN: You can even tell the guards, we'll drive away fast.

PAT: You did them, you did the murders didn't you? Tell me you did them and I'll let you go.

JOHN: Yeah. We did them. Let us go.

PAT: You can't go, your brother is dying. He can't walk. I'll let you go.

(JOHN looks at TOM.)

JOHN: Try and get to your feet.

(TOM shakes his head. JOHN tries to lift him to his feet.)

TOM: I can't. *(Showing him the blanket now soaked in blood.)* Look.

PAT: *(To JOHN)* Are you going?

(TOM looks at his brother again.)

TOM: Don't leave me here.

JOHN: I can't carry you.

TOM: Don't go, John.

PAT: I'm giving you your life.

JOHN: *(To TOM)* I might be able, I might be able to do something if I went...I might be able to get help.

TOM: No. Look at the blood...look at the blood. Don't go.

JOHN: Why didn't you fucking duck or something!

TOM: I'm dying, John.

JOHN: Don't keep talkin like you're in a fuckin' video. *(JOHN quickly gets to his feet and goes to the door.)*

TOM: No! No! Stay with me, John.

JOHN: *(At the door.)* I'll get help.

TOM: No! No! Stay! Stay!

(JOHN has his hand on the door handle. He opens it.)

TOM: John.

(JOHN quickly turns around and comes back in. He slams the door. He bangs his fists against the wall.)

JOHN: Fuck it! Fuck it! Fuck it! *(He takes the picture of the old men's parents and throws it against the wall, shattering the glass. He turns and looks at his brother, tears in his eyes.)*

(PAT is watching all this. He still sees JOHN as a murderer, but he now also sees him as something else. A member of a family carrying the guilt and obligations of blood ties.)

DAN: Are they gone?

(JOHN looks at PAT.)

JOHN: You knew. You knew I couldn't do it.

PAT: No. I didn't know. I didn't know.

(JOHN goes over to his brother and puts his arms around him. TOM is slipping into a coma. He closes his eyes as JOHN

takes his hand. PAT is standing in the middle of the floor, years of government forms at his feet. DAN is sitting in his chair looking straight ahead.)

PAT: That's the curse. That's the curse. It's your own flesh and blood. The fondness. You stay because of the fondness. Not a thing you can do about it. Even if you went as far as China.

(JOHN stands up and looks at PAT.)

JOHN: My brother is dying. Don't even know where I am. I'm going to kill you.

PAT: What did you kill all them people for? Tell me! Tell me! Tell me! You don't know who you're killing. I can't understand it.

JOHN: You stabbed my brother. You didn't know him.

PAT: He was your brother. *(Holding up his bandaged hand.)* And you drew my blood. And the blood of my neighbours. You couldn't have done worse, you couldn't have done worse in this county of dead lines. Did you go to school? Did you?

JOHN: School.

PAT: Did you?

JOHN: Yeah.

PAT: Did they teach you about the great famine?

JOHN: Fuckin' mad bogman.

PAT: Did they teach you about the famine?

JOHN: Yeah. Yeah.

PAT: Well you know then. That makes it worse.

(PAT looks at the knife in his hand, then looks away. He stares at JOHN, then quickly goes over to him and holds the knife to his throat.)

PAT: Should kill you now.

JOHN: I promise we'll never come this way again.

PAT: Kill you for all the bad things that was done to us.

JOHN: I'm only young.

(PAT isn't listening to JOHN. He is staring deep into his eyes.)

JOHN: Let me go.

PAT: It was like someone somewhere, far away, made up his mind we were to die out.

(JOHN stands, shell-shocked by what has happened to his brother and the fury of the old man. Still holding the knife, PAT gets down on his knees and starts to gather up the old forms, almanacs, etc. He takes an old yellowing form and looks up at JOHN.)

PAT: Do you know what this is? The rates, a rate bill. *(Reads)* "Paid with thanks. May 1958." *(He gathers up some more forms. Still on his knees, he holds up a fistful of forms in JOHN's face.)* Paid with thanks. Every year, every single year. Owing no one nothing. That was the way in all the tins and cardboard boxes you scattered to the wind. *(He throws the forms to the ground and looks up at JOHN. PAT then looks over at TOM.)* What age was he? Twenty years ago.

JOHN: Eighteen. He wasn't born.

(PAT takes away the knife.)

PAT: He wasn't born. Lying there like a beast in the field.

(As PAT looks down at TOM, he is trying to make some sense of the fact that he has possibly murdered someone who wasn't even born when his own body started to break down. Thinking these thoughts, he is off-guard. JOHN seizes the opportunity. He gets behind PAT and, after a brief struggle, gets the knife. PAT is lying on the ground, near TOM. All around him is a mess of old forms, calendars and almanacs. JOHN kicks the mess to one side and stands over PAT.)

DAN: What's happening?

PAT: I was taking pity on him.

JOHN: Least we live in the fuckin' times we're livin' in. Get up and get yer money.

(PAT gets up.)

PAT: *(Laughs)* It's more than money now. Look at that knife you're holding, that's your brother's blood! How can you ask for money? *(PAT looks at the blood-stained blade.)* That's his blood! Your brother's blood!

JOHN: Get it and I might let you have a quick death.

PAT: If I could put some nature into you...That's his blood, eighteen years of it...that's his blood.

(JOHN is staring at PAT.)

JOHN: Shut the fuck up! Crap talk comin' outa ya all night. *(JOHN looks over at DAN who is still sitting in his chair.)* Fuckin' mad house. Why did we have to come to this fuckin' mad house! *(JOHN goes and picks up a milk bottle, brings it over to TOM.)* I had a dream once, when I was goin' to school. About two old men in a room, one of them blind. And I was outside, walkin the land. *(JOHN looks around him. He is feeling displaced. He almost forgets that he is holding the knife. He stares at DAN.)* We spent the whole of the fuckin' winter going from door to door. House to house. The stuff was crap and everyone knew it. You can't fool people. They know it all, from TV programs. Shows about rip-offs. They look at your face and all they see is a balaclava from the TV.

(He attempts to give TOM a drink from the milk bottle.)

JOHN: Tom.

(PAT looks over at DAN.)

PAT: Dan.

(PAT goes over to DAN, then draws in closer to him.)

PAT: Dan.

DAN: That's the first time you said my name in twenty years. They were only selling blankets.

PAT: You haven't seen the wildness that's abroad out there.

DAN: What wildness?

PAT: Lorries that are bigger than a house. Drums blasting from shop doorways...and the young...the young dressed like they're in some war.

DAN: They're brothers.

PAT: Killers.

DAN: You said you'd bury me alive.

PAT: That was talk! That was talk! That was, family...family talk.

DAN: You said —

PAT: That was family —

DAN: You were going to lock —

PAT: Family talk —

DAN: Me in the mental —

PAT: I said! I said! I only said it, I never did it, did I?

DAN: Every day, every time I want to listen to the foreign station you say you'll lock me in the mental.

PAT: That's only talk!

DAN: I believe it.

PAT: Only talk!

DAN: I'm a frightened man for many a year. Frightened of you, Pat and the power you have over me.

PAT: I'd never have done it, Dan. You know I'd never have done it, don't you? *(PAT sees the picture of his parents that JOHN hit against the wall. He picks it up and shakes away the pieces of broken glass from the frame.)*

DAN: It wasn't because of me you stayed.

PAT: No. It wasn't. There was the land, the family...I had reason.

DAN: I'm not mental. It was a terrible sin for you to hold that over my head. That was cruelty.

PAT: But it was only...

DAN: I hear the key turn. They're locking me up. Taking away my radio. I hear it every time you talk. Every time you turn off the foreign station!

PAT: The foreign station! There's a mad child holding a knife over us and you talk about the foreign station!

DAN: You know that station is my salvation. All the other wireless talk is like you in the evenings. Talk about trouble and days for lockin doors. When I listen to the foreign station I know there's a world out there.

(JOHN has been watching the last bit of this conversation. PAT looks at TOM.)

PAT: That boy is on his way out.

JOHN: Tell me where we are.

PAT: What? What are ya askin' me?

JOHN: Tell me where we are so I can get outta here.

PAT: And leave your brother half-dead on the floor.

JOHN: You can look after him.

DAN: God help him so.

PAT: Your heart is gone to stone.

JOHN: Tell me where we are.

PAT: I look into your eyes and I see nothing. No past, no people, no land.

(JOHN gets up and moves in closer towards PAT.)

JOHN: Big talk. From a man who's lived on tinned peas for the past hundred years.

PAT: There was once more than tinned peas in this house!

JOHN: When will ya get it into yer thick culchie skull that once is worth fuck all!

PAT: There was cattle and sheep, pigs. Stock on the land.

JOHN: Don't be listin' your dead stock to me. Give me the money.

PAT: I'll give you nothing. *(Picks up an old rate bill.)* The cows and bullocks I took to market had more feeling and history in their eyes than you ever will. Your face is a calamity from the Sunday newspaper.

JOHN: Where are we?

PAT: What begat you? What begat you?

(On the floor, TOM stirs and groans.)

JOHN: If he died in this house.

PAT: He'll not be the first to die in this house.

JOHN: Killed by an old man's talk.

PAT: My father and mother were waked in this house. My grandfather was laid out on that table. But you aren't from any country I know. *(PAT is looking straight into JOHN's eyes now.)*

PAT: Go over to your brother. He's on the way out.

(JOHN goes over to TOM again.)

JOHN: Tom, Tom..think you can walk now?

(PAT laughs quietly.)

PAT: Where were you reared?

JOHN: Tom? *(John puts more blankets over Tom's shoulders.)*

PAT: If them that built this house saw this night. A child's blood comin', wrapped in a blanket the colour a the rainbow.

JOHN: Bogman, for the love a Christ, no more talk.

33

PAT: You'll have to hear it. I was born in this room *(Looks over at DAN.)* He was too. Winters, summers, things that came and went. Stories about wars that were on far away. Letters from America, forms from the government. Tales of terrible things going on outside...wars in China. What did we know about wars? We only heard the stories, the stories of terrors far away. Soldiers killed in the Congo. Hacked to death. Terrible things done to missionaries. President Kennedy shot in America. *(PAT takes the radio in his hands.)* They were terrible stories. Terrible, terrible happenings. But in the end, in the end you could sleep at night. And in the morning this place would still be here, sun shining or rain falling, cows in the field. And whatever story we heard yesterday, about the terrors outside...we'd forget it in time. It was the same when the North started. Bombings, "only next door we used to say". But we could still sleep at night. And after a while, after a while it was as far away as the Congo. We laughed at Paisley and that crowd. It was hard to feel anything for all that. It was only when we heard stories of bad things happening to one man or woman...Kennedy's blood on Jacqueline's dress. That was terrible. But it was so far away. It was all wireless talk. *(He places the radio in DAN's lap)* Wireless stories.

(JOHN breaks the spell that PAT has cast over him. He takes a rate bill and sets it alight. He drops it into a bucket.)

JOHN: It's all going to go up in flames.

(PAT is still staring at him. JOHN takes another old form and sets it on fire. PAT suddenly picks up a bundle of old forms and notices. He holds them to his chest. JOHN keeps setting forms alight and throwing them into the bucket. PAT takes an old yellowing calendar and looks at it.)

PAT: Tides. Holy days and Bank holidays. What did we keep them for anyway? Every year. Was it my mother who started keeping them? Or was it me? *(He takes a rate bill.)* Rates. Rates..poor law..paid in full. *(He sees the old booklet "Bás Beatha". He takes it and looks at it.)* "Bás Beatha." This came in the post in 1966. Telling us how to stay alive when the bomb was dropped. We were supposed to keep it in a safe place. Always have it handy so that we'd know what to do when the war started. *(Looking through the booklet.)* "Have the radio by your side...put sandbags against the door." Sit in a safe corner under the table when the big war comes. Bloody government. They never told us about the real terrors to come. *(Takes some old forms.)* Brucellosis testing. TB. The vet will call...general election... referendum...dog license. For a dog's been dead for forty years...there's nothing here that matters. Why did we keep them?

(JOHN takes the bundle. PAT goes over and stands behind DAN.)

PAT: They said, they promised us it was always going to be the same...they told us to keep the old ways...and we did. We did! We did keep them, we did keep them, did like we were told. *(Pause)* And what harm, what harm blanket-seller but we had it in us...we had it in us to be heaven and earth.

(PAT goes over and takes a bundle of forms. He throws them into the blazing bucket. They burn. JOHN still stands holding the bundle of calendars and almanacs PAT thrust into his hand. PAT looks at JOHN. It is no longer a stare. JOHN bends down slowly and throws the bundle into the bucket. TOM starts sobbing again. JOHN goes over and sits by his side. He takes the blanket and puts it around his own shoulders. PAT stands by the blaze coming from the bucket, occasionally throwing in another form or calendar. They all look like refugees from some war. After a time, DAN switches on the radio. The French announcer is introducing a piece of music. The lights fade as the music from Europe plays and the forms and calendars of a lifetime burn.)

END

THE MARLBORO MAN

A One-Act Play

Clare Dowling

The Marlboro Man was first produced by the **Project Arts Centre** in September 1994 with the following cast:

WANDA	Donna Dent
MICK	Conor Mullen
DJ	Paul Kehoe
WOMAN	Clare Dowling

Director   Conal Morrison

PLACE

The Curragh Army Camp

TIME

Present Day

THE MARLBORO MAN

The set is a one-bedroom flat in run-down army living quarters. A single door leads off to the hallway and communal bathroom. The kitchen area is in one corner of the room, cramped and basic. The small living space is managed well, but the potential is there for chaos. Startling touches of glamour provide some relief — colourful clothes spill from the dressing-table drawers, a pile of cuddly toys sits on the double bed, a film poster decorates the wall. An army uniform in dry-cleaning plastic hangs from a hook. A stereo-radio takes pride of place on top of the dressing table. The radio conversations of the DJ and the WOMAN are pre-recorded. Some extra background music and/or chat should be recorded to fade in or out as needed.

The set is in darkness. There is a soft, insistent snoring from the bed. Suddenly, an alarm shrieks shrilly. It is viciously slammed off. WANDA catapults herself from the bed and stumbles across the room towards a light switch. Lights up.

WANDA turns on the radio, where a love song incongruously plays, then hurriedly sets about her morning ablutions. She pulls on a dressing gown, picks up clothes from the floor, grabs a can of cat food, sets up the ironing board, crawls on all fours looking for the cat, peeks out the door, plugs in the iron and puts on the kettle. MICK snores on, oblivious.

The song on the radio gives way to a signature tune. WANDA immediately turns up the volume, then swoops onto a stool in front of the dressing table and examines her appearance in the mirror. Diligently, she searches for wrinkles, for blemishes, for grey in her hair. She attacks her eyebrows with a tweezers.

DJ: *(In a mid-Atlantic accent)* Good morning to you —

WANDA: Morning Declan —

DJ: Hope you're all in good form this morning —

WANDA: Didn't sleep a wink —

DJ: Let me see it's just coming up to ten minutes past nine —

WANDA: It's not, is it?

DJ: Declan Neary here with you until noon. I'll tell you, there's something going on out there that I don't know about —

WANDA: What's that?

DJ: We got over seventy calls in response to the show yesterday, can you believe that?

WANDA: Seventy!

DJ: Seventy and rising and in the light of that we've decided to scrap what we had planned for the show today and take it up where we left off yesterday. Already we've had Marion from Celbridge on the line, who doesn't believe that married women have affairs out of boredom. If you're bored, she says, there are any number of night classes —

WANDA: Ha!

DJ: Well now Marion, I think that —

DJ: You're missing the point.

WANDA: *(In unison)* You're missing the point.

DJ: And for those of you who would like to make an intelligent comment, our phone lines are open on 6677720 and in response to Paula's call yesterday we'll be talking about legal separation, more about that later but first the usual parish announcements... roadworks on Inchicore Road, traffic at a standstill, Dublin Corporation are either digging the road up or putting the road down, we're not quite sure which, but it's a job that can only be done in rush-hour traffic on the

Friday morning of a bank holiday weekend but thanks for the warning, Dublin Corporation...

This galvanises WANDA. She turns down the radio, goes to the bed and shakes MICK.

WANDA: Mick! Mick, get up! Get up, will you! There's roadworks on the Inchicore Road!

He surfaces with a coughing fit. She goes back to her eyebrows.

WANDA: *(To audience)* You should have heard the program yesterday, it was incredible. Frances from Terenure rang in and said that she's been married for ten years but has been having an affair with her boss for the last five. He just looked at her over the photocopier one day and said that he was mad for her and to hell with the consequences. To hell with the consequences! She fell for him on the spot, she said. That got the whole country going, I can tell you. But I know how she feels. I fell for Mick on the spot when he roared up on his motorbike outside our unisex hairdressers, in a leather jacket and with a cigarette hanging out of his mouth at just the right angle. I was so nervous that I gave him a perm and Mrs Dwyer a short back and sides by mistake. To hell with Mrs Dwyer! Mick said, and we ran out of the hairdressers and jumped into bed. It was just like what happened to Frances from Terenure. Except that Mick never actually said that he was mad for me, but I could tell by the look in his eye.

Sound of helicopter flying low overhead.

WANDA: They're starting that racket early, aren't they Mick?

He myopically lights a cigarette.

WANDA: Mick, there's roadworks in Inchicore. We'll never get there on time.

MICK: We'll go in the back way.

WANDA: And will you ever get up? How can you just lie there and you after setting the alarm wrong again?

MICK: I didn't set the alarm. You did.

WANDA: And you shouldn't be smoking in bed. One of these nights, you're going to burn the whole place down.

MICK: You started me on them.

She waves imaginary cigarette smoke out of her eyes.

WANDA: It's disgusting, that's what it is —

MICK: *(Mimicking)* Smoking at this hour of the morning —

WANDA: Absolutely disgusting. I dread to think about the state of your lungs — ouch! Now look what you made me do — I'm after taking too much off the left.

She flings down the tweezers and examines her eyebrows.

MICK: At least now they match.

WANDA: That's a terrible thing to say, Mick. I could have taken out one of my eyes.

MICK: Ah, sorry Wanda.

WANDA: And what're you apologising for? It wasn't your fault, was it? You spend your whole life apologising lately. *(Pause)* Mick. Mick, what do you think they'll say?

MICK: I don't know, Wanda. There's no use asking me again. We'll just have to wait and see.

WANDA: And get that cigarette away from me! It took me ten years to give 'em up and I asked you not to be tempting me!

She gets up from the dressing table. He sits down in her place.

WANDA: I can smell the drink off you from here. Well I hope you're sorry this morning.

MICK: Course I am. I wouldn't want to disappoint you.

WANDA: Sylvester! Where are you! Pshwisshhh wissh!

He starts to put in contact lenses. She searches about for the cat, extinguishing his cigarette as she goes.

WANDA: Disgusting, that's what those things are. Sylvester!

MICK: *(To audience)* The last time I felt this rough was after we lost the Cup Final in May. Myself and Wanda sat up until four in the morning bad-mouthing the ref. It was just like the old days, when we'd be watching football in the pub on a Saturday afternoon. She'd drink whiskey and smoke Marlboros and curse like a truck driver. Then home and we'd stay up all night discussing bodywaves and rinses and how long it took for my perm to grow out. I thought she was a fluke until I met the rest of her family that first Christmas. I stood in the corner with my mince pie while they all drank whiskey and burned cigarette holes in the carpet and shouted each other down. "He doesn't say much does he?" I remember the mother screaming across the room at Wanda. So I had a whiskey and a cigarette just to fit in and when I woke up they were still going strong. It took a lot more whiskey and cigarettes to get to sleep last night.

His last words are drowned out by the buzz of a lady's electric razor.

WANDA: *(Defensively)* There's someone in the bathroom. Probably your man from upstairs, Private Callaghan —

MICK: Cullinan.

WANDA: Whatever, he's always in there for hours. It'd be lovely to have our own bathroom.

MICK: I'm working on the transfer. I've told you, it takes time.

WANDA: Declan says the first sign of an affair is when people start taking more care of their appearance, spending time in bathrooms. I wonder if Private Cavanagh's at it.

MICK: Cullinan, Wanda. Cullinan!

WANDA: Whatever. Anyway, a transfer wouldn't make any difference. It's always couples with no kids that they stick in places like this. Isn't it Mick?

MICK: We were just unlucky. Here, did you not get any cornflakes?

WANDA: I got muesli instead.

MICK: Fucking Bombay mix.

WANDA: It's better for you. I remember you telling me. You said people with kids get the half-decent houses. People like us get dumps like this.

MICK: You remember too much.

He eats his cereal. Sound of helicopters again, louder.

WANDA: I don't know why they have to start that racket so early.

MICK: Because it's their job. Lucky bastards.

WANDA: Mick, will you ever get dressed? I got your uniform dry-cleaned day before yesterday.

MICK: I'm not going in my uniform.

WANDA: But you look so nice in it! Especially now that they sewed on those little stripes that say you're a corporal. Jesus, Mick, at the rate you're going you'll be a general soon.

MICK: And I'll still be sitting behind a desk.

WANDA: Sylvester! Look what I've got for you! Rabbit liver and heart, yum yum. Mick, I can't find Sylvester. Did you do something to him?

MICK: Not yet.

WANDA: Don't mind Daddy, Sylvester. He's a bit off today.

MICK: I am not his Daddy.

WANDA: See? He is a bit off.

MICK: Jesus, he's a cat, Wanda!

WANDA: I know that. There's no harm in pretending.

She starts to iron a garish blouse, dosing it with starch.

WANDA: *(To audience)* I wouldn't blame Sylvester for hiding. He doesn't like it here in the Curragh. When Mick decided to join the army, I had visions of going along with him on top-secret missions and getting into the VIP stand at

Croke Park. I never in my wildest dreams thought I'd end up on the wrong side of Naas. I remember the day we arrived, and asking the army wives what the place was like. Soldiers, sheep and shite, they said. I bawled my eyes out on Mick's shoulder and he went and swapped his Kawasaki for a second-hand Lada so he could take me back to Lucan at weekends. I knew how much he loved that motorbike, so I'd send him off to the barracks every morning with a smile and a kiss and then I'd be screaming down the phone to my mother about how bored I was. "And how's Mick?" she'd ask, "has he spoken yet?" Then she'd say isn't it a grand life I have all the same, when she was my age she was trying to feed six. "Wait till you have two under the age of three," she'd say, "and then we'll see how bored you get."

She turns up the radio.

DJ: And thanks to Teresa for that comment and we're delighted you've come through your affair smiling, but unfortunately, not all husbands are as understanding as yours — especially when it comes to their golf partners. Now, what time have we...

WANDA: Twenty-past-nine.

DJ: Just coming up to twenty-minutes-past-nine and we have Catherine — is it Catherine? — yes, Catherine on the line from Wicklow, now Catherine has not actually had an extra-marital affair, but her husband has — and this is quite an extraordinary story — Catherine, good morning to you.

WOMAN: Hello? Hello, Declan?

DJ: Hearing you loud and clear Catherine.

WOMAN: I don't know if the line's great —

DJ: Catherine, you are the wronged party here, yes?

WOMAN: Sorry?

DJ: Your husband was the one who did the dirt on you, so to speak.

WOMAN: Oh he did, Declan. He did the dirt for over two years before I caught him at it.

The action continues over the radio around this point.

DJ: Red-handed, so to speak.

WOMAN: But I'll tell you one thing, Declan, he'll never do it again.

DJ: That's what our listeners want to know, Catherine, is there any way of ever trusting a wayward partner again?

WOMAN: Well, I don't know about trusting them —

DJ: Live with them, then? Continue with the marriage?

MICK: Do we have to listen to that rubbish?

WANDA: It's not rubbish. Declan talks about things that nobody else wants to talk about.

She turns the radio up very loud. They shout over it.

MICK: Nobody wants to listen to it either.

WANDA: No, I think that's just you, Mick.

MICK: What? Will you turn that thing down!

WANDA: What did you say?

MICK: I said, will you ever —

She turns it off. Oblivious, he continues shouting.

MICK: Turn that fucking thing down!

WANDA: There's no need to shout, Mick.

Sound of machine gun fire, close. She dives dramatically to the floor.

WANDA: (*Defensively*) Sergeant Carey's wife told me last week that a bullet from the range came through her window in 1989 and hit the TV. What're you laughing at?

MICK: They were only winding you up.

WANDA: I knew that. I was just... practising.

MICK: I can't believe you were taken in again. After the time they told you I was missing in action in Newbridge.

WANDA: They don't like me.

MICK: Oh come on, it's just their way of going on. You have to toughen up, Wanda. Just tell 'em all to fuck off.

WANDA: I don't fit in, I have nothing in common with them.

MICK: You should join one of those clubs they've set up. Get out more.

WANDA: You can talk.

MICK: What?

WANDA: Dropping out of the darts league.

MICK: I told you, I didn't drop out, I was dropped.

WANDA: I had Sergeant Morrissey around here the other day accusing me of keeping you from playing.

MICK: Fed up of darts.

WANDA: You never go into the mess anymore. You never go into Naas. You never set foot outside of this place unless you absolutely have to. I hope you're not staying in on my account.

MICK: Has it occurred to you that I might be staying in on my own account?

He gathers shaving things and starts to shave over a basin of water.

MICK: *(To audience)* I applied to be a pilot in the Air Corps just after we got married and failed the medical. They said my eyesight was so bad they'd think twice about letting me up as a passenger. They told me, "Better try the army, son, they'll take anything." I got the contact lenses then and for the first time ever, I could actually see Wanda coming before I heard her. She worked overtime in the hairdressers to pay for the flat in Portobello while I trained as recruit No. 843231. We were so broke that first year that our social life revolved around the bed. The day I became a One Star Private, she shot fourteen rolls of film and posted copies to all the newspapers, before dragging me into the hairdressers in my uniform to show the girls. We were trying to fiddle a mortgage application the morning the transfer came. It's only for a couple of months, they said — that was three years back.

Sound of helicopters again.

WANDA: Wonder what's going on.

MICK: There's someone coming down from Dublin. Official visit.

WANDA: Who?

MICK: I don't know.

WANDA: Yes you do. You just won't tell me.

MICK: Wanda, please don't ask me, it's —

MICK: Classified information.

WANDA: *(In unison)* Classified information.

WANDA: You never tell me anything anymore. I used to tell you all about my job in the hairdressers. Remember the time I cut the hair of that minister's wife? I knew the government was going to fall before anybody else did.

MICK: Here, when are you going to get me some new gossip?

WANDA: Don't start that again, Mick. Not this morning of all mornings.

MICK: You've been putting off going back for months now. And don't give me that rubbish about it being too far away.

WANDA: Well it is.

MICK: You could commute, like thousands of others. You can't let your whole life hang on what they tell us today, you know. We have to go ahead and make plans, regardless. Remember they told us to do that?

WANDA: It's easy for them to tell us what to do.

MICK: Supposing it's bad news?

WANDA: Mick!

MICK: It might be, Wanda, face facts for once. And if — if, mind — it is, wouldn't it be better for you to have a job to go to?

WANDA: It's easy for you, you've got your high-flying career.

MICK: Oh, so you mean I'll be fine, while you mope around making me feel miserable for keeping you down here? What kind of a plan is that?

WANDA: Am I making you miserable?

MICK: We're calling into the hairdressers today and you can have a chat with Anne Marie. See about getting your job back.

WANDA: I'll think about it.

MICK: We're calling in, okay? *(Cuts himself with razor)* Shit.

WANDA: *(To audience)* We won't call in to the hairdressers and talk to Anne Marie. He's always threatening to, but I'll put him off. Instead, we'll go out to Lucan and watch Blind Date and listen to my Ma insulting Cilla Black in one breath and asking me why I'm not pregnant in the next. Then my sister Martina'll drop over with her husband and the four kids in tow and nobody'll bother with Mick and me for the rest of the evening. Martina had to give up her job for good after she was caught out with the third and she's been moaning about it ever since. Myself and Mick used to visit, and when we'd see the mountain of filthy nappies and the four of 'em swinging out of her, we'd look at her with pity. We'll wait a few years, we said, and live a bit first. After a few more years, she started to look at us with pity. "Still," she says to me, "aren't you lucky in a way, isn't your life your own." Mick says that between her and my mother, my family are the most tactless people he's ever met.

She turns on the radio.

DJ: Now let me get this straight, Catherine... you actually followed your husband to his mistress's apartment —

WOMAN: That's right.

DJ: And threatened him with his own shotgun. I can't believe this. And what did you do then, Catherine?

MICK: Don't answer him Catherine.

WOMAN: I stood there and looked at the pair of them in that bed, and I just got so angry that I lifted that shotgun and I pointed it at them... and I — I —

DJ: Yes, Catherine?

WOMAN: I — sorry about this — I couldn't decide whether to shoot him or her first and then myself afterwards, or whether to shoot myself first and then... *(Very upset)* Sorry about this, I don't think I can go on...

MICK: Shoot Declan first, Catherine, then shoot yourself.

DJ: You just take your time, Catherine, we going to ease up a little here and we'll be right back to you after this, stay tuned.

The chat show gives way to music. WANDA furtively starts to dress, using her night-gown as a shield. Finally, she is forced to discard the night-gown, revealing a bra. She fumbles quickly into the newly-ironed blouse but the arm of the blouse is tangled.

MICK: It's inside out.

WANDA: What?

MICK: The sleeve. It's inside out.

WANDA: Oh, right.

MICK: Here, let me —

WANDA: I can dress myself, thanks!

MICK: *(Rapidly retreating)* Okay, okay. Sure you're half-dressed anyway. Don't know what you wear a bra to bed for.

WANDA: Marilyn Monroe used to, once she hit her thirties. That's when everything starts to fall down and shrivel up.

MICK: One of these nights you're going to strangle yourself.

WANDA: *(Nervously)* Mick, what're you standing looking at me for?

MICK: Am I not allowed to look at you anymore?

WANDA: Course you are, don't be silly... Mick, what age would you think I was?

MICK: Twenty-eight.

WANDA: Tell the truth now.

MICK: Twenty-seven.

WANDA: Mick!

MICK: Twenty-six?

WANDA: I wish. Your eyesight must be getting worse. Is this blouse a bit much, do you think?

MICK: No. Makes a nice change from those jeans and T-shirts you're always in these days.

WANDA: Yeah, well they're comfortable. God, I'm a mess without my make-up, amn't I? No wonder you never said you were mad for me.

MICK: Everything has to be said out loud with you, Wanda. You don't believe anything until you actually hear it.

WANDA: And how else am I supposed to believe it? By your actions?

MICK: Don't give me that. You're the one who wears your underwear to bed.

He moves off and lights another cigarette.

MICK: *(To audience)* She never even used to wear perfume to bed and then the underwear started appearing. I knew there was something up the day she went out and bought me new underwear. I thought it was in case I got knocked down and put it out of my mind. Then she started mentioning gynaecologists and clinics and how lucky we were to have the Lada for the trips to Dublin. I didn't want to hear about it back then — we'd have kids sooner or later without some doctor interfering. I gave in after eighteen months and that's when it all started — sneaking out on my days off on the pretext of going shopping; ringing the clinic up on the public phone; pretending to her parents that we visit so often because we like them. From the start, I warned her not to be telling the world and his mother once she got a couple of drinks in her down the pub. We said we'd only talk to each other about it. But on the mornings we'd be going to Dublin, we'd sit over the cornflakes watching each other in silent suspicion. The only reason we stay up nights now is if there's a good film on the telly.

WANDA: Look at you. You're not even dressed. Anybody would think you didn't want to go.

He takes a shirt from the laundry basket and starts to iron it.

WANDA: Here, I'll do that.

MICK: No, it's fine, I can do it myself.

WANDA: Do you think I'm incapable of doing anything anymore?

MICK: Course not, it's just that I always do my own shirts... Here. You do it. You do 'em much better than me anyway.

She sprays starch wildly on his shirt. He takes a pair of jeans from a drawer.

MICK: *(Mutters)* Jesus Christ.

WANDA: What's wrong.

MICK: Nothing, nothing at all. Nice and crisp, these jeans.

WANDA: *(Pleased)* Yeah?

He holds up the jeans. There are two rigid creases ironed down the middle of the legs.

MICK: You could get paper cuts off these.

She flings down the iron.

WANDA: Do it yourself.

MICK: Ah Wanda, I was only joking.

WANDA: Maybe you'd like to put my make-up on for me? I'm bound to put on too much.

MICK: Wanda, don't be like that. You know bloody well that I was only slagging you. Can you not take a joke anymore?

WANDA: Course I can. Sorry. Now, Mick, let go of me, would you please? I'm trying to put on my make-up. And can you hurry up, please?

MICK: No. I have to put those jeans on slowly in case I break 'em.

He continues to iron his shirt. She liberally applies make-up, then turns the radio up.

DJ: And you'd do it while he was at work? That's a bit childish, Catherine. And I really don't think it'd make you feel any better.

WOMAN: I think I'd feel a lot better, even if it is childish, Declan. And he was always so bloody proud of that greenhouse, going on about his tomatoes and his cucumbers and his prize-winning squashes. Do you know, I think he spent more time talking to those squashes than he ever did to me. All I need is one stiff frost.

DJ: But surely things are acrimonious enough without this kind of thing, wouldn't you say?

WOMAN: And whose fault is that?

WANDA turns down the radio.

WANDA: *(To audience)* I hope she does ruin his squashes, whatever they are. It's good to let your anger out, the doctor said. I tried throwing a glass into the fireplace like they do in the films, but it didn't break. It was one of those plastic ones that only look like glass, and I took it out on Mick instead. Sometimes I go into Naas on my own for the day just to let him recover. I stand in the supermarket eating free sausages off one of those stands and watching the pregnant women going past. Once or twice I've followed them just to see what they're going to buy. It's amazing how they all seem to go shopping the days I go into Naas. They're at the bus stop, in the post office, queuing in front of me at the bank. Even the girl behind the counter is in a smock. I tried to give up my seat on the bus for another one day. She laughed and said that she must be putting on weight. She wasn't pregnant at all.

MICK goes to the door and peers furtively out.

MICK: *(To off)* Oh. Morning. No, no you go ahead.

He dodges back in.

MICK: That bastard has gone back into the bathroom — Cullinan. What does he be doing in there at all?

WANDA: Why did you let him go in ahead of you? He's only a private, you're a corporal, you must be entitled to some privileges.

MICK: Ah, didn't want to make a fuss.

WANDA: I've heard it, you know.

MICK: Heard what.

WANDA: Your nickname. The Marlboro Man. And the jokes about shooting blanks.

MICK: I can handle them.

WANDA: Course you can. That's why we're barred from two pubs in Naas.

MICK: One pub. Ah Jesus, I didn't do anything last night, did I?

WANDA: No. You insisted that we sit out in the beer garden, remember? You said the lashing rain was refreshing. Had nothing to do with the fact that a crowd of them were sitting in the lounge.

MICK: Did you see them? They were laughing at us, Wanda. Laughing their fucking heads off!

WANDA: They were watching telly. They were paying no attention to us.

MICK: To you, maybe. It's me they're laughing at. And it's me who has to go out and face them every morning, you know.

WANDA: I know that, Mick.

MICK: Ah, what do they matter anyway? Nothing better to do, eh?

WANDA: Course they matter. But you'd want to be careful. You don't want to be getting into trouble. They won't like that if any of it gets back.

MICK: I won't be getting into trouble.

WANDA: The only reason you didn't last night was because I was with you. I don't know what you get up to when you go out on your own.

MICK: I don't be 'getting up' to anything, as you put it.

WANDA: You could always tell them, Mick. Get it out in the open, it'd be easier on you —

MICK: No. It's none of their business.

WANDA: They're going to find out sooner or later. If you don't tell them, I will.

MICK: No.

He goes to the door, opens it and roars out.

MICK: Will you ever hurry up in there! There's other people want to use the fucking bathroom too, you know!

He storms back in and lights a cigarette.

MICK: What are you looking at me like that for? Well?

WANDA: No reason.

MICK: That's the only way to get him out. No consideration, that bastard.

She starts to do her hair, liberally dosing it with hairspray.

MICK: *(To audience)* Sometimes I can hardly face walking out of here in the mornings to the smirks and the pitying looks and the jokes in the canteen. Can't get away from it — I gave up the darts because of commiserations about my aim being off; I walk into the canteen and someone starts whistling the tune to Blankety Blank; walk onto the rifle range and they all duck. Fuckers. The worst is having to tell my lads what to do — ten teenage recruits standing there trying to keep the smirks off their faces. One of 'em gave me a compass for Christmas and I made him scrub toilets for three weeks. One morning, I walked into the barracks to find my locker plastered with pictures — filth from those magazines — tore them all down and they were back up by lunchtime. I demanded a transfer. "What do you want a transfer for?" said the company sergeant, winking across at the lads, "you're getting on here, aren't you?" Bastard turned me down flat. Tell them, she says. But I can't.

WANDA: Mick, I've changed my mind. I'll have a drag after all.

MICK: You will not. I'm not supposed to be tempting you, remember?

WANDA: I've decided I was too harsh on you. Give me that cigarette, Mick!

MICK: No. You don't need one.

He extinguishes the cigarette, drops to the floor and does press-ups.

WANDA: You're right, Mick. You go ahead and smoke your head off in front of me and then tell me I don't need one.

MICK: Sorry.

WANDA: There you go again. Apologising. What are you apologising for, Mick?

MICK: Three. Four.

WANDA: We used to have some great bloody fights, remember? Now all you do is say sorry.

MICK: Wanda, will you just give over now, please.

WANDA: 'Give over'. There was a time when you would have told me in plain and simple terms to shut up.

MICK: Shut up, Wanda!

WANDA: Thank you!

MICK: I didn't mean shut up... I meant... just leave it, Wanda.

WANDA: No. No, thank you for treating me like you used to treat me. And will you stop doing those bloody exercises and look me in the eye for once in your life!

MICK: Wanda, I'm nervous too. Will you stop trying to pick a fight.

WANDA: Fighting is better than nothing. You were never a great one for the idle chat. Especially when you've got a hangover.

MICK: Is that what this is about? Me getting drunk last night?

WANDA: No! Yes! Mick, we're going to find out from the doctors today and instead of talking about it last night like normal people, we end up in the beer garden of the Horse & Carriage in Naas.

MICK: Well it was better than sitting here apologising all night!

WANDA: Nobody's asking you to apologise.

MICK: What are you asking me to do then? There was a time, Wanda, when you'd have a drink with me, a time when you'd be sitting up in the bed chattering on, instead of pretending to be asleep.

WANDA: They told us not to be drinking and smoking.

MICK: Those doctors are taking over our whole fucking lives, do you know that?

WANDA: I've listened to enough of that kind of talk, Mick. Why can't you for once say something positive?

MICK: But that's just it, Wanda. You see, you don't want to talk reasonably about it. All you want to hear is me reassuring you that it's all going to be fine and that the news will be just great today. Well I'm not going to bury my head in the sand with you, not when we don't even know. The only thing we can hope for is that there's a chance.

WANDA: Why couldn't you have said even that much to me last night? Why, Mick?

MICK: Why couldn't you have said it to me? Why is it always me who has to bolster you up? You think I don't want to believe it as much as you? I want kids too, you know.

WANDA: I know.

MICK: It'll be the same for both of us in there today.

WANDA: In a way. Only in a way. Now we'd better get moving or we won't get there at all. Sylvester! I'm leaving your rabbit liver and heart on the floor for you and if you don't come out in three seconds, I'm going to eat it myself.

She opens the can and puts the contents into a bowl.

WANDA: *(To audience)* He can be desperately negative sometimes. I didn't tell him, but I tried to sign us both up for the birthing classes in Naas that start in November, but they won't accept you until you're actually pregnant, imagine that. They wouldn't take my word for it. But I believe the doctors when they say there's a chance. The first doctor we went to was desperately negative too, and that's when I persuaded Mick to look for a second opinion. Well, you'd look for a second opinion too if you were hearing the words 'dysfunctional' and 'deficient' and 'irregular'. Half of them I had to look up in a dictionary. Don't know why I bothered, they all mean the same thing — you're not normal. I got real angry with that doctor, even though he was only doing his job. But he was wrong, I know he was. He said we could always look for a second opinion, so that must mean something mustn't it? He might be a doctor but they get it wrong sometimes too.

She checks her watch and panics. She starts stuffing things into her bag — keys, tissues, etc.

WANDA: You're going to have to wear your uniform, Mick.

MICK: What?

WANDA: What with the traffic and those roadworks and it being Friday, it's the only way we're ever going to get parking. Official business and all that.

MICK: I'm not pulling that one again.

WANDA: It works, doesn't it? Please, Mick. If we miss this appointment, we won't get one for weeks and weeks and I'll be back on the smokes if that happens.

He takes the uniform from its hook and starts to put it on. She takes a pile of leaflets from a folder.

WANDA: Did you read all this stuff.

MICK: Yeah.

WANDA: It's amazing what they can do with people nowadays, isn't it, Mick?

MICK: Depending.

WANDA: Absolutely amazing. You've any number of options. If this particular part of you is dysfunctional, then you can try this drug here. And if that part of you there is crocked, then there's always this treatment here. If all else fails, then you can go to this place in Boston where the Americans have an answer for everything.

MICK: Now stop that, Wanda. It mightn't come to any of that.

WANDA: True. They might tell us to forget it altogether. Mightn't they, Mick? Being negative.

MICK: Being realistic. Then there's always this one here.

He picks up a leaflet.

WANDA: No.

MICK: You haven't even read it.

WANDA: I don't need to. We'd be years on a waiting list. I'm not putting in any more years, and all for someone else's? No.

MICK: What about me? You're ruling it out on my behalf as well, are you?

WANDA: Sorry.

MICK: I'm surprised I'm being allowed to go at all today.

WANDA: For God's sake, Mick —

MICK: But if they tell us no this morning, Wanda, I'm not going with you to any more doctors. We could be years clutching at straws and wasting time on treatments that don't work and then find it's too late for anything else.

WANDA: Sylvester!

MICK: Wanda, did you hear what I just —

WANDA: Mick, I think we should get rid of Sylvester. You heap love and affection on him and he turns around and disappears without even telling you where he's going. Sylvester? Will you please come out?

MICK: Wanda. Open your eyes! He's not here! The cat is not fucking here!

She turns away and continues her preparations.

MICK: *(To audience)* I feel like I'm at one of those horrible funerals where you never know what to say. I'm afraid that I'll turn around in a minute and tell her that I'm sorry for her troubles. I nearly did the day those first results came back and we knew for certain that it wasn't me. It's getting to the stage now where I wish it was. I'd call a halt to the madness — the doctors, the false hopes, the whole bloody thing. Then again, maybe I'd do exactly what she's doing, and if there's half a chance... Christ, I wish someone would write a few leaflets for those of us on this side, to tell us what to say or do. The day Wanda went looking for a second opinion I went drinking on my own in Naas. Sat there eyeing up women at the bar. I fell home to find Wanda waiting up for me, all excited about this new doctor who she thinks can walk on water. I hope he can.

WANDA: Are you ready to go.

MICK: You haven't eaten any breakfast.

WANDA: I don't want any.

MICK: Will I make some tea?

WANDA: No.

MICK: Toast?

WANDA: No. I'm fine.

MICK: You have to eat something.

WANDA: Mick, I don't want tea or toast, all right? Next thing you'll be offering me two aspirin.

She abruptly turns on the radio.

DJ: My God, the switchboard is literally jumping, the comments are coming in thick and fast... Mary says that what Catherine did was understandable but that violence never solves anything... Joe says that quite frankly he thinks she's making it all up... Yvonne very strongly suggests that Catherine is unstable... she also gives us a stern warning about the effects of television and says that an incident like this would never have happened in this country back in the days of radio... and finally William has rung in to ask Catherine does she know she needs a license for a shotgun... oh dear, there's always one, isn't there... fourteen minutes to ten o'clock, we'll go back to Catherine, if we still have her —

MICK turns off the radio.

MICK: Can't bear that stupid chatter in my ear.

WANDA: It's not stupid chatter. You just didn't want to hear what they were talking about.

MICK: Wanda, I don't care if Catherine shoots the Pope.

WANDA: You know what I mean — marriages breaking up and all that kind of thing. That's one option we didn't discuss.

MICK: They didn't give us a leaflet on it.

WANDA: But you must have thought about it.

MICK: No.

WANDA: I have.

MICK: What?

WANDA: Yes, Mick, me. Or had you ruled that one out on my behalf? I'm not going to hold you to anything. You think I'd be happy living like that? Course I've thought about it. And you're a liar if you say you haven't.

MICK: But we don't even know yet —

WANDA: It doesn't matter if we know or we don't. You must have made your decision by now. I wouldn't blame you, you know, if you wanted to go. Like the doctors said, it's not your fault. Now, I'm going to take a cigarette from that packet and I'm going to smoke the whole damned thing. Okay?

MICK: I'll get you a light.

WANDA: *(To audience)* I will smoke this cigarette. And I'll go on smoking. And if the news is bad today, I'll go out and buy a crate of whiskey. What does it matter now? We'll go and sit in that waiting room and Dr Kennedy'll ask if we've discussed the pros and cons and possibilities and options and we'll say "Yes, doctor," and he'll open his file and give me the results of all those weeks of tests. And if the results are good, if I have a chance, Dr Kennedy will smile and say wasn't it all worth it. And if the results are bad, if there's no chance at all, he'll tell us that the most important thing is to think of the future. And Mick and I will look at each other and I'll wonder if we'll be thinking of the same one. Mick?

MICK: I can't find the lighter —

WANDA: Mick, I'm dreading this.

MICK: I know. Me too.

WANDA: I haven't been this nervous since I got my Leaving Cert results. I failed that too.

MICK: So did I.

WANDA: Did you? You never told me that.

MICK: Thought I did. Yeah, five F's and a B.

WANDA: You big liar. Five B's and an F.

MICK: Shite.

WANDA: What do you think they'll say, Mick?

MICK: What do you want to hear, Wanda?

WANDA: Sorry.

MICK: There's a chance. That's all. But it's better than nothing.

WANDA: Yes. Mick? I might stay in Lucan tonight — depending. I'm not saying you have to come with me — where's that shagging lighter — you can come back here if you want.

MICK: Ah, you're not going to leave me sitting up all night on my own?

WANDA: All right. You've twisted my arm.

He finally unearths the lighter.

MICK: Thank Christ. Here.

WANDA: Naw.

MICK: I thought you were dying for one.

WANDA: It took me ten years to give them up. I'm not going back on them now. But you go ahead.

MICK: Right. Thanks. Well, maybe not. Disgusting really, smoking at this hour of the morning.

After final preparations, they go to the door. MICK stops, as though hearing a noise.

MICK: Bet that little bastard's been here all along. Sylvester! We're going now. Eat your breakfast, don't go outside and don't be leaving hairs on the bed. *(To WANDA)* Will he be all right, do you think?

WANDA: Jesus, Mick, he's only a cat.

They leave, closing the door behind them.

Lights down.

END

GREATEST HITS

A One-Act Play

Thomas McLaughlin

Greatest Hits was first produced by the **Project Arts Centre**, Dublin, on the 24th of May 1994, with the following cast and crew:

JOHN	Barry Barnes
BOBBY	Michael McElhatton
Director	Eamonn Hunt
Stage Manager	Rónán Ó Muirgheasa
Lighting	Paul Keogan

TIME

Present

LOCATION

A Room

GREATEST HITS

The set is a nondescript room, with a table, two chairs, a sideboard and a radio-cassette player. BOBBY sits at the table. JOHN stands at the opposite end, rooting in a plastic bag.

JOHN: Did you have lunch?

BOBBY: No.

JOHN: Yeah. Sorry about the short notice, but, you know? I got one of the young lads to pick up something. *(Takes out cellophaned sandwich and peers at it)* And this is...looks like...egg in...vomit actually. Egg mayonnaise. Fancy it?

BOBBY: No thanks.

JOHN: Don't blame you. And this is... *(Takes out another cellophaned sandwich and looks at it)* This is another egg mayo.

BOBBY: I'm not very hungry.

JOHN: I know what you mean. Still. *(Beat)* You sure you won't have a beer?

BOBBY: No thanks.

JOHN: Ah come on Bobby. Have a beer for God's sake!

BOBBY: I don't want a beer John. Alright?

JOHN: *(Beat)* Fair enough. *(Beat)* I won't tell anyone.

BOBBY: Tell anyone what?

JOHN: That you had a beer.

BOBBY: I didn't have a beer.

JOHN: Well, if you had one I wouldn't —

BOBBY: I'm not going to have —

JOHN: Hey look, it's no big deal.

BOBBY: I know it's no big —

JOHN: Then let's forget about it. *(Beat)* OK? *(Beat)* Relax.

BOBBY: I am relaxed. Don't I look relaxed?

JOHN: Yeah. Yeah, you look good.

BOBBY: Well, that's good. Considering.

JOHN: Considering what?

BOBBY: Considering I shouldn't be here.

JOHN: *(Beat)* You want to leave? There's the door.

BOBBY: This is a serious breach of protocol John. Serious.

JOHN: Ah come on Bobby! We're just having lunch!

BOBBY: Lunch.

JOHN: Lunch! Food you eat in the middle of the day. Lunch! Very civilised I'm told.

BOBBY: *(Beat, looks at watch)* So this will take...what? The traditional...hour? The executive forty-five minutes?

JOHN: *(Annoyed)* Let's be mad bastards and go the full hour. *(Beat)* Like the old days. *(Beat)* Lunch and a chat like normal people. You and me.

BOBBY: *(Beat)* I suppose sometime during this hour you'll tell me what this is really all about.

JOHN: Were you always this suspicious?

BOBBY: Yes.

JOHN: *(Beat, smiles)* Yeah, you were weren't you! *(Starts to unwrap sandwich)* I think I'll chance one of these salmonella sarnies. Life's one big risk, isn't it?

BOBBY: So I hear.

JOHN: *(Grins)* You sure you don't want a beer?

BOBBY: I'm sure.

JOHN: Not like you.

BOBBY: I've changed.

JOHN: *(Reaching into plastic bag)* So I hear.

BOBBY: Oh? From who?

JOHN: *(Taking a can of coke out of the bag)* What?

BOBBY: Hear from who?

JOHN: Hear from who what?

BOBBY: That I've changed.

JOHN: No, just that you'd gone off the drink.

BOBBY: Who'd know?

JOHN: What?

BOBBY: Whose business was it?

JOHN: It's nobody's business.

BOBBY: I was never on the drink, OK?

JOHN: I never said you were.

BOBBY: Somebody else say it?

JOHN: No, they said the opposite.

BOBBY: *(A little confused)* What?

JOHN: That you were off it.

BOBBY: *(Beat)* I was never on it. OK? *(Beat)* I gave it up a year ago.

JOHN: Yeah, well. That's what I heard. So I got you this. *(He hands the coke to BOBBY)*

BOBBY: Then why did you ask me if I wanted a beer?

JOHN: Maybe my information was wrong. Or maybe lack of drink messed up your brain and you'd forgotten you were on the wagon.

BOBBY: *(Slight smile)* Jesus!

JOHN: God Bobby, don't lose the run of yourself, you nearly smiled there. *(Takes a can of beer out of the bag and opens it)* So. Cheers. *(Drinks. BOBBY doesn't. Beat)* What?

BOBBY: I only drink diet coke.

JOHN: You're kidding!

BOBBY: What?

JOHN: You're not fat.

BOBBY: Because I drink diet coke. And I only eat once a day.

JOHN: That's not natural Bobby.

BOBBY: When you're older your metabolism slows down. Weight goes on and doesn't come off.

JOHN: When you're older, Bobby. Not now.

BOBBY Now is older John.

JOHN: *(Beat)* It's a young man's game right enough. *(Beat)* You do get tired don't you. *(Beat)* Don't you?

BOBBY: *(Beat)* Am I being retired?

JOHN: You want to be?

BOBBY: Is this what this is about?

JOHN: Sure they wouldn't send me.

BOBBY: Maybe to break it to me gently?

JOHN: *(Beat)* You want out?

BOBBY: And do what?

JOHN: *(Shrugs)* Teach? Some of the young guns. They might reach your standard.

BOBBY: Can't teach it John. Can't learn it. You just...have it.

JOHN: And how do you know when you've lost it?

BOBBY: That's the trick.

JOHN: *(Smiles, offers coke)* You sure you don't want it? *(BOBBY shakes his head)* You'll fade away.

BOBBY: Might come in handy.

JOHN: True enough. *(Beat, drinks beer)* You know what I was thinking about?

BOBBY: What?

JOHN: Remember the poteen we made thon time in Tripoli?

BOBBY: Yeah.

JOHN: In the bath. And what did you call that wee nurse?

BOBBY: Pauline.

JOHN: Pauline! God! That's right. From Birmingham. She thought it was water. She got into the bath! *(Beat)* And then she hit me with her handbag, remember? What was that all about?

BOBBY: Because you said you wanted to suck her dry.

JOHN: I just didn't want to waste the drink.

BOBBY: I don't think she realised that.

JOHN: I told her it was nothing personal.

BOBBY: That's when she hit you.

JOHN: *(Laughs, drinks, beat)* She had the hots for you. I screwed it up. Sorry. *(Beat)* And then we drank the poteen!

BOBBY: We figured Pauline wasn't dirty. Because she was a nurse.

JOHN: *(Laughs, beat)* Women! Sure who knows? *(Beat, BOBBY smiles)* Oh I got something. *(JOHN gets up)*

BOBBY: What?

JOHN: *(Goes to radio-cassette on sideboard)* Just talking about Tripoli there. Listen to this. *(Switches on the tape)*

BOBBY: What is it?

JOHN: Wait, wait, wait. *(The music starts — Marvin Gaye's 'I Heard It Through the Grapevine')* All right! OK, come on Bobby, what is it?

BOBBY: Ah yeah, it's —

JOHN: Not the song, that's easy. The album! *(Sings along with the song)*

BOBBY: It's Greatest Hits.

JOHN: Nearly.

BOBBY: It is Greatest Hits.

JOHN: Chartbusters.

BOBBY: Chartbusters, same thing.

JOHN: No it isn't. And what else?

BOBBY: What?

JOHN: What else?

BOBBY: *(Beat)* Ah yeah! Number...

JOHN: Volume!

BOBBY: Volume...3!

JOHN: Yes! Alright! *(Sings along a while, fades, beat)* Tripoli all the same.

BOBBY: *(Beat, remembering)* Yeah.

JOHN: Forty shades of sand. No drink. No women. More or less.

BOBBY: No distractions.

JOHN: Ah well, you liked it. You were good at it. *(Beat)* Remember your man wore the thing on his head? Reminded you of the tablecloth in your granny's? Bit of a fanatic?

BOBBY: Raschid.

JOHN: The very man. Rat Shit. First time we met I says to him, "Jesus, look at all this sand, when does the cement arrive?" Not a flicker, not a smile, nothing.

BOBBY: Might be the way you tell 'em.

JOHN: Ah no. No sense of humour.

BOBBY: Different culture John.

JOHN: Ah but he knew from my tone I was telling a joke. He might have, you know, give us a smile out of politeness for God's sake.

BOBBY: We weren't there to have fun.

JOHN: Them boys were serious right enough. *(Beat)* Sort of wasted on me.

BOBBY: You did all right.

JOHN: No...I just...I couldn't...

BOBBY: You had other talents that's all. You just weren't suited to that end of it.

JOHN: Sometimes I wish I was.

BOBBY: What?

JOHN: Out in the field. Out where it's happening.

BOBBY: It wouldn't suit you Johnny. You're better off here.

JOHN: Co-ordinating publicity? Co-ordinating tea breaks more like! What is it today? Hobnobs? Or will we have the chocolate digestives? No, wait wait wait — executive decision — lemon puffs! Or does that conflict with historical precedent? Is that the image we want to promote? Well...let's play it safe and go back to the Hobnobs! *(Beat)* Back to the...I tell you Bobby, you know what I'd like to go back to?

BOBBY: What?

JOHN: Cushendall.

75

BOBBY: Cushendall?

JOHN: *(Beat, smiles)* Cushendall. *(Beat)*

BOBBY & JOHN: Susie McCormack! *(Beat, they laugh)*

JOHN: Been there lately?

BOBBY: Cushendall?

JOHN: Or Susie.

BOBBY: Susie got married.

JOHN: Did she?!

BOBBY: Couple of years ago. Some American. She lives in the States now.

JOHN: You serious?

BOBBY: Yeah. I got a Christmas card. Albuquerque.

JOHN: Albuquerque! You never know where you're going to end up. *(Beat)* Except of course, we're going to end up here.

BOBBY: Our choice.

JOHN: We'd no choice. Not really. Not after Tripoli. *(Beat)* So. You been to Cushendall lately?

BOBBY: No. No point.

JOHN: Suppose not. *(Takes a bite out of his sandwich. The egg mayo squirts out)* Gah! Glamourous eh? Business lunches!

BOBBY: What business?

JOHN: What?

BOBBY: What are we here for?

JOHN: No no no, no business today. No I just thought the other day "God, I haven't seen Bobby in months. We should get together." You know how it is. You lose touch.

BOBBY: Things change.

JOHN: Oh yeah, of course. But I think you need...I don't know...some kind of personal contact. Otherwise you might start thinking you're all alone.

JOHN: Is that what you think?

JOHN: What?

BOBBY: That you're all alone?

JOHN: Well...no more than yourself.

BOBBY: Comes with the job.

JOHN: Well...I suppose. But at least you're independent. Back at headquarters...I just follow orders.

BOBBY: I'm not independent. I follow orders too. Just like you.

JOHN: Yeah, but you got nobody breathing down your neck, you can use a bit of imagination, a bit of initiative. As long as the work gets done who cares how you do it? I don't. Headquarter! Policy! Toe the line! Follow the strategy!

BOBBY: You have a problem with that?

JOHN: *(Beat)* Not at all. I'm a good boy. I do what I'm told.

BOBBY: So do I. *(Beat)*

JOHN: Susie McCormack. *(Beat)* Remember the time —

BOBBY: Johnny!

JOHN: What?

BOBBY: *(Opens can of coke, toasts)* Here's to you and here's to me and if by chance we disagree.

JOHN: *(Beat, realises, continues toast)* Screw you, here's to me. *(They grin and drink)* You're a wild man all the same. *(Beat)* How's Annie?

BOBBY: I don't see her anymore.

JOHN: Ah no. Since when?

BOBBY: Almost a year.

JOHN: A year?!

BOBBY: Almost.

JOHN: I must have seen you since then. You never said.

BOBBY: We were working.

JOHN: Yeah. Yeah. *(Beat)* That's a pain in the arse. I liked Annie. *(Beat)* So what happened?

BOBBY: She wanted kids, I didn't. End of story.

JOHN: Yeah, right. *(Beat)* Maybe you'll change your mind.

BOBBY: *(Beat)* Kids are a liability. *(Beat)* How're your two?

JOHN: They're great. Getting big now.

BOBBY: Yeah they must be.

JOHN: Last time I met you — socially — was the christening. That must be...Jesus...nearly two years!

BOBBY: Yeah. Almost. Can you tell them apart yet?

JOHN: Only if I look in their nappies. And you can only look at your kids' genitals up to a certain age before you're a pervert. *(Beat)* No, Robert's a bit bigger and a bit darker. Kate's a wee angel. Robert's supposed to look like me.

BOBBY: Poor bastard.

JOHN: Watch it! *(Beat)* You should come visit. Let the poor child see his godfather.

BOBBY: *(Wry)* It's kind of difficult.

JOHN: I know. *(Beat)* Still at least you send good presents. His Auntie Maggie sent him a bible! *(Beat)* But you should come. I mean, we named him after you.

BOBBY: *(Smiles)* Yeah yeah, sure you did.

JOHN: We did!

BOBBY: Celia told me that she called him after Robert De Niro.

JOHN: Ah yeah, but I didn't object, and I always had you in mind.

BOBBY: And Kate was called after.

JOHN & BOBBY: Kathleen Turner!

JOHN: Kathleen Turner.

BOBBY: Your squeeze.

JOHN: Ah yeah, Kathleen Turner, yeah, I like her. "Into the mud, scum queen!" *The Man With Two Brains*? You see that?

BOBBY: No.

JOHN: She was great in that! Lots of underwear. Steve Martin, you know?

BOBBY: I don't really see films.

JOHN: *Body Heat*? See that? Kathleen Turner as well. Celia and I were courting when we saw that. Fairly steamed up her Da's Cortina afterwards.

BOBBY: So you named your children after film stars. Have you no tradition!

JOHN: Could've been worse, we could have named them after...game show hosts...Cilla and...I can't think of anyone else.

BOBBY: Then there's hope for you yet. *(Beat)* So. Things are OK?

JOHN: Things are great. Kids are starting to chat. Well, making noises that sound like chat. They know what they're saying even if I don't. I discovered that Robert says no when he means yes. Like — "Do you want a sausage Robert?" "No." "Well, do you want some toast?" "No." "Then what do you want?!" "Sossie." That means sausage so it's "I asked you if you wanted a sossie and you said no, now do you really want a sossie?" "No!!!" And then Kate, when she says yes she goes "Hmmm." Like she was saying "What?" So that's "Do you want a sausage?" "Hmmm?" "Do you want a sausage?" "Hmmm?" "A sausage! Do you want a bloody sausage?!!" So both the kids are starving right? Robert thinks his da is mad, offering him all this food and then never giving him any, and Kate thinks I'm stupid and, like, don't understand plain English. So they look at me like..."Who is this eejit?!" *(Beat)* Celia understands them. *(Beat)* Maybe I'm not with them enough.

BOBBY: How is Celia?

JOHN: Grand. *(Beat)* Well...doing all right, considering. You know? The job.

BOBBY: Aye well. That's why I didn't want kids.

JOHN: Yeah but you know, everything's a risk these days, you might as well —

BOBBY: John! You're...an administrator. Desk job. Don't get me wrong, I'm not saying anything, that stuff is necessary. But out on the streets, on the front line, actually doing the business! You can't be thinking about sausages and toast and nappies and screwing Kathleen Turner, you have to be clear! You know what I'm saying?! Clear! Nothing between you and what you have to do! Moving forward, moving forward all the time, moving forward, all the time one step ahead of the other guy. *(Beat)* You don't know what it's like. The board doesn't know what it's like. Nobody does. Except the people doing it.

JOHN: Ah now hold on a minute Bobby, I think I have some idea —

BOBBY: You think!!

JOHN: Yeah! I think. And if I think it, maybe it is it! A lot of it's in your head, that's what you said once, it's in your head, your approach, your attitude.

BOBBY: Is that right?

JOHN: That's what you said. *(Beat)* Yeah. I think I could have done it. Given the chance.

BOBBY: Really?

JOHN: Yeah! Really!

BOBBY: Ask the board for a transfer.

JOHN: Pah! Some chance. *(Beat, drinks)* I could go out with you.

BOBBY: What?

JOHN: On a job.

BOBBY: I don't think so.

JOHN: Who'd know?

BOBBY: I would.

JOHN: But nobody else!

BOBBY: *(Beat)* You know John, you always did talk shite.

JOHN: *(Beat, laughs)* Yeah. But what the hell, eh? I'm only talking to you. *(Finishes can, gets another out of the bag)* Anyway, shite is in the ear of the beholder. *(Opens can and drinks)*

BOBBY: You should take it easy.

JOHN: Relax. It's only beer. *(BOBBY looks at his watch)* Will we play "I Spy"?

BOBBY: It's your party. *(Beat, JOHN sings along with the tape)*

JOHN: Have a beer for Gods sake!

BOBBY: I said I didn't want one.

JOHN: For old times' sake.

BOBBY: What's the matter Johnny? You got no one else to drink with?

JOHN: No one like you. No one I know.

BOBBY: You don't know me John. You know...some young guy, Cushendall, swimming at night. The first taste of poteen, both of us chasing a girl called Susie —

JOHN: You won.

BOBBY: Some American won. *(Beat)*

JOHN: You won. I knew you would.

BOBBY: John. Forget it. Kids' stuff. Dead and buried.

JOHN: You know how I knew you'd win? Because you'd got...what's the word? Tunnel vision! Tunnel vision! You see something, you go for it. No distractions. *(Beat)* I got distracted. *(Beat)* Wife. Kids. Mortgage. A stupid dog that won't fetch. Car on its last legs. *(Beat)* It's not what I thought Bobby. It's not what I planned, you know?

BOBBY: We don't make the plans John.

JOHN: Yeah yeah. *(Beat)* Sometimes I think there is no plan. *(Beat)* It's the kids. What happens when they get older? Start asking questions? What am I going to say to them?

BOBBY: They'll make their own minds up John.

JOHN: I thought this place would be sorted out by now. *(Beat)* You know what I saw the other day? I was on this bus, right? I was going into town and we stopped at these traffic lights. And this other bus pulls up beside us, right? So I glance over, just a look, the way you do, and I saw, directly opposite me this wee lad, about five or six, at the window, just about... two feet from me. And he was in tears, these big tears just rolling down his cheek. So I kept on looking, you know? And there's this woman sitting beside him, mid-thirties, kind of good-looking, blonde hair like the wee lad. And I remember thinking "Ah, that's his mother" but not, and I remember, not because their hair was the same but because she was shouting at him. I couldn't hear her of course but you could tell she was shouting. Her face. And there was no one else on the bus with them, upstairs. So she was going on at this wee lad and he was crying away and then, all of a sudden, she punches him! I mean...punched, you know? I mean, wasn't a slap or anything, she really leant into it WHAM! back of the head, you know? And his face smacked into the window, right? Right up against the glass, just across from me, face on. And...I don't know...I wanted him to...hit her a dig, or...be angry or...shocked or... *(Beat)* But he didn't look anything. He was like...gone. Out like a light. I couldn't believe it. The wee boy was

82

unconscious! *(Beat)* Then the lights changed and the bus moved on. *(Beat)* It took about... five seconds. *(Beat)* And I couldn't do a damn thing. Just watch this...And then. *(Snaps his fingers, beat)* Everything moves on. *(Beat)* I don't know what made me think of that.

BOBBY: Kids.

JOHN: Oh. Yeah. They break your heart, Every time. Mine'll do it to me. I know it. *(Beat)*

BOBBY: You know Tony?

JOHN: Hmmm?

BOBBY: My sister's lad, Tony.

JOHN: Margaret's boy

BOBBY: Yeah.

JOHN: How is Margaret?

BOBBY: Ach, could be better.

JOHN: Oh, is Jack still...?

BOBBY: Yeah.

JOHN: That's a shame.

BOBBY: Yeah. Anyway, Tony got himself...drugs.

JOHN: Ah no.

BOBBY: The serious stuff.

JOHN: That's terrible.

BOBBY: Anyway, Tony was in a bad way, robbing from the house and everything and God knows Margaret hasn't much worth taking. Jack's drunk most of it. *(Beat)* So anyway she asked me if there was something I could do about Tony. Talk to him or something. *(Beat)* She said he looked up to me.

JOHN: I'm sure he does.

BOBBY: Yeah well. So, I got a couple of the lads and we hoisted Tony off the street one day, stuck him in a car, blindfolded him and took him off.

JOHN: I'd say that fairly shook him.

BOBBY: He was shitting himself. I mean, literally. In his trousers.. *(Beat)* The lads had done the whole business — balaclavas, anoraks, the full regalia. *(Beat)* The smell! *(Beat)* So anyway, we took him to this house out in the country a wee bit. Sort of farm.

JOHN: Oh the one in —

BOBBY: Where we had the —

JOHN: I know the one. The Germans?

BOBBY: Yeah. So we put Tony in a room and take off the blindfold and of course as soon as he sees me it's "Jesus Uncle Bobby! What's goin' on? What's goin' on?" and "Uncle Bobby" this and "Uncle Bobby" that, and the two lads in the balaclavas are cracking up, you know? Uncle Bobby! So I says to Tony "I'm not your uncle! I'm not your family. Heroin's your family and until you quit it, you're nothing to me!" *(Beat)* Then the lads dragged him outside and you know those Corporation workmen's huts? That don't look like huts, they look like big metal containers?

JOHN: Yeah.

BOBBY: We took Tony and stuck him in one of them that was out in the yard, and I say, "Tony, welcome to the turkey farm." Cold turkey, yeah?

JOHN: Yeah.

BOBBY: (Beat) People are animals, you know? When you get right down to it we'll beg and scream and howl with the best of them. Tony — Jesus! He cried like a baby and then he whined like a dog — "Uncle Bobby, Uncle Bobby please, please Uncle Bobby." *(Beat)* And then he started screaming. *(Beat)* Four days. Altogether. *(Beat)* More shit. And piss. And puke. *(Beat)* Four days. That's how long it took. Don't know how long it took for Tony, probably seemed like years. The lads looked after him when I wasn't there.They'd hose him down when he dirtied himself. *(Beat)* I'd hold his hand, you know? And talk, anything really, any ould nonsense. Sing sometimes. Just to let him know he wasn't alone. I don't even know if he heard me. *(Beat)* I told him I was doing it because I loved him. I tried to make him understand that that's what all this pain and fear and...filth was about. Love. *(Beat)* I didn't hate him. I don't hate anybody.

JOHN: *(Beat)* Did it work?

BOBBY: He was clean when I'd finished.

JOHN: Did he stay clean?

BOBBY: Don't know. Little fucker ran away. Nobody's heard from him in months.

JOHN: I tell you, kids have no gratitude.

BOBBY: And of course Margaret blames me. Won't have me in the house anymore.

JOHN: You did your best.

BOBBY: Maybe I should have minded my own business.

JOHN: It was your business.

BOBBY: Was it?

JOHN: You made it your business. *(Beat)* You made it your business — that's morality. *(Beat)* You do your best you do your best and you get shit for your trouble. Or no one even notices you. *(Beat)* Just trying to make a future for our kids and nobody gives a damn anymore. Nobody cares. Everybody's just..."Oh one day at a time, don't expect anything we'll struggle on." I mean, a young lad on drugs or somebody gets killed — so what?! It's "Oh it's the Troubles." "It's Northern Ireland, sure they're all mad bastards there!" I mean, who would you have to kill so that people get outraged?! Who?! Who would you have to kill?!

BOBBY: *(Beat)* Kids.

JOHN: No no no that's not outrage that's, like...tragic. No, I'm talking about something that's just...senseless! You know? So senseless that people go "My God! This crap has got to stop because that was so...senseless!" Who would you have to kill?

BOBBY: I don't know.

JOHN: Think!

BOBBY: I don't know!

JOHN: Ah come on, who? Who would you have to kill?

BOBBY: I don't know John!

JOHN: *(Beat)* Pick a name out of the phonebook? Drive around taking potshots?

BOBBY: Look, you want to play games, let's play "I Spy" like you said. This is stupid!

JOHN: The problem is that people wouldn't know you'd picked them out of the phonebook, they'd think there was a method, and then whoever you hit is going to be one side or the other so people automatically think it's sectarian. So that wouldn't be senseless. Or appear to be.

BOBBY: *(Beat)* Supppose you hit a...Buddhist or a Hindu or whatever.

JOHN: Then you think "What the fuck are they living here for?!!" Mad bastards brought it on themselves! Bad karma man. Serves them right. *(Beat)* Or you hit...like, second cousin of a dentist once drilled...Edward Carson's great-grand-nephew's teeth, and there you are, that's reason enough to blow the guy away. That's still not senseless.

BOBBY: So everyone's a legitimate target.

JOHN: Seems like it. And so nobody gives a damn. *(Beat)* What about somebody...good?

BOBBY: Good?

JOHN: Like Mother Teresa, only from here? Non-sectarian, appeals to both sides, a decent human being.

BOBBY: *(Considers)* Somebody good?

JOHN: *(Beat)* I can't think of anyone.

BOBBY: *(Beat)* Nor me.

JOHN: *(Beat)* George Best!

BOBBY: George Best?

JOHN: Geordie Best!

BOBBY: *(Considers)* George Best.

JOHN: George Best, man of the people, loved by both sides.

BOBBY: But is he good?

JOHN: Far as I'm concerned he's better than Pele.

BOBBY: *(Smiles)* I don't know about that.

JOHN: Yeah, well, you're a Spurs fan, so...you know? *(Beat)* You still follow them?

BOBBY: TV. Now and again.

JOHN: *(Beat)* Ah but you see, George is a Prod, so it'd still be sectarian. No, we need somebody not connected with the North.

BOBBY: What, we go overseas?

JOHN: Well, shooting people in like, Luxembourg, would be senseless right enough, but that's a bit too far away. No they have to be here, but not from here.

BOBBY: Journalists? *(Beat, they dismiss journalists.)* Yeah.

JOHN: Yeah, who'd care? *(Beat)* Tourists?

BOBBY: Sure who'd want to come here?

JOHN: Hey! The Antrim coast! Cushendall! Forty shades of green. It's a great wee country.

BOBBY: Saints and scholars.

JOHN: Exactly. *(Beat)* Tourists.

BOBBY: OK.

JOHN: But they can't be English.

BOBBY: Or Americans. That'd be like pissing in our own wallet.

JOHN: Or any Arab types. They might be our friends. Who knows? They all look the same. OK, Europeans then.

BOBBY: *(Beat)* The French?

JOHN: Well, everybody would like to kill the French!

BOBBY: Germans?

JOHN: Six million Jews? *(Beat)* What about the Swiss?

BOBBY: The Swiss?

JOHN: The Swiss. *(Beat, considers)* I mean, what did they ever do for anybody? Or to anybody? The Swiss! The anonymous Swiss. The neutral, blameless, keep-themselves-to-themselves Swiss! I mean, if serial killers went after countries, it'd be Switzerland they'd be following up the alley with the blowtorch! The Swiss! I think they're our boys!

BOBBY: So...we wait for an international yodelling competition in the Ulster Hall?

JOHN: We don't have to. They're here.

BOBBY: *(Beat)* What?

JOHN: Conference of Swiss schoolteachers. Staying in the Franklin Hotel. Going to the Giant's Causeway tomorrow, all packed neatly in a big bus. Forty of them.

BOBBY: *(Beat)* Jesus Christ!

JOHN: Let's talk business.

BOBBY: You're serious!

JOHN: Just hear me out.

BOBBY: Lunch is over.

JOHN: Listen to me Bobby.

BOBBY: I don't think so John. I think we should forget this meeting ever took place!

JOHN: It never did. Officially. This is just between us.

BOBBY: There is nothing between us.

JOHN: We're friends. *(Beat)* I need your help. *(Beat)* Come on please Bobby, sit down. Sit down, please. Just hear me out. For old times' sake. *(Beat. BOBBY sits)* OK. People get killed. Why? The Troubles! It's like we said — they were connected in some way, I don't know, they must have been, everyone is, we're all legitimate, you said it yourself. *(Beat)* It's dull. It's become dull. *(Beat)* But what would grab people's imagination? Eh? *(Beat)* Random violence! *(Beat)* Random violence! Kid in the supermarket, the ma looks away, five seconds, BANG! Kid's sliced in two in a dustbin. Or Bosnia? What's that all about? Guy two legs blown off at the knee, news camera at the stumps — Serb? Moslem? Croat? Who knows? People are going "What the hell is going on?" Ninety people incinerate themselves for Jesus and you know what that does? Makes people think about Jesus and then about why he lets that happen and then they think about the devil and then they think they see evil walking about in the world. Evil! Rearing up on its two hind legs and walking about in the world! *(Beat)* And why? Why does all this stuff happen? *(Beat)* Why?

BOBBY: *(Beat)* Are you asking me?

JOHN: Yeah.

BOBBY: How the hell would I know?!

JOHN: Exactly! Oh sure, we can all make up reasons — they're sick bastards, God told them to, they saw a video. But the thing is, the thing that really scares the shit out of people is that no one really knows. *(Beat)* No one knows. "Why me? Dear God in heaven, why me?"

BOBBY: *(Beat)* What are you saying?

JOHN: That we should go with whatever's happening! The mood of the...times. Whatever...fear and despair there is out there, we should be using. They're tools for God's sake!

BOBBY: To do what?

JOHN: To build a better future for our kids!

BOBBY: By killing a busload of Swiss?

JOHN: *(Beat)* I don't hate anybody either Bobby.

BOBBY: *(Beat)* You shouldn't be saying this.

JOHN: I trust you Bobby. I think you understand. *(Beat)* We're friends.

BOBBY: And as a friend I'm saying I didn't hear this. Forget it John.

JOHN: *(Beat)* Let me ask you something Bobby, just between me and you. The shopping mall, the bank, couple of projects before that. Your projects. Very profitable, very efficient, very...clean. Except. *(Beat)* People were killed.

BOBBY: *(Beat)* What people?

JOHN: Nobodies. Irrelevant. Nothing to do with us, nothing to do with them. Collateral damage.

BOBBY: So?

JOHN: So it's a coincidence. Right? Except coincidence is only coincidence until you start to look for a pattern. Until you find it.

BOBBY: I don't know what you're talking about.

JOHN: It's just this thought came into my head. "Bobby killed those people."

BOBBY: You're insane.

JOHN: But then I thought "Why? Why would he do that? That's...senseless." *(Beat)* Battle fatigue? Shellshock, post traumatic whatever the hell they call it these days? Well...that's a reason. That's legitimate. In a war. So then I said, "OK, the war killed those people." And I thought that was terrible Bobby. That the thing we were supposed to be controlling was controlling us. I felt sick. Not at you. At the world. At the one we made. *(Beat)* I felt sick.

BOBBY: You are sick.

JOHN: Maybe we're all sick.

BOBBY: *(Beat)* Have you said any of this to the board? Because I tell you John, they'll think you're crazy and they'll retire you. And you know how.

JOHN: And I thought, the guy that's killing them, what does he feel?

BOBBY: Maybe it was six different guys. Maybe there is no pattern. Maybe you made it up. Maybe you are sick.

JOHN: Maybe I am. *(Beat)* Maybe I am. *(Beat)* But suppose I'm not. Suppose I'm right. *(Beat)* I mean, you're out there Bobby man. You're out there on the edge. I mean, you're right. I don't know what it's like. I'm not judging you. You have instincts, you go with them. That's what makes you good. That's what we want. That's what I want. That's what I need!

BOBBY: *(Beat, starts to get up)* Thanks for the lunch.

JOHN: Come on Bobby, sit down.

BOBBY: I think you're sick John.

JOHN: Then you go to the board. *(BOBBY starts to go)* Or why don't we both go to the board. *(BOBBY stops. Beat)* See what happens. *(Beat)* You see, the thing is, Bobby, you knew how many murders there were.

BOBBY: What?

JOHN: In this pattern that may or may not exist. You knew how many.

BOBBY: How would I know?

JOHN: See, that's what I mean. *(Beat)* You told me six.

BOBBY: I didn't tell you anything.

JOHN: Yes, you did. A while ago. You said it could be six different guys. How did you know?

BOBBY: I didn't know. I just picked a number.

JOHN: But how did you know it was six?

BOBBY: I didn't.

JOHN: You said it.

BOBBY: I guessed.

JOHN: Good guess. Dead on the nose.

BOBBY: Jesus Christ!

JOHN: So how did you know?

BOBBY: For God's sake John —

JOHN: How did you know?!

BOBBY: *(Beat)* Is this room bugged?

JOHN: *(Beat)* I need bodies. I need someone who can give them to me. Someone who understands. *(Beat)* I need you Bobby. *(Beat)* Look I don't know why you killed those people, maybe you don't either but...we're friends. *(Beat)* We should help each other.

BOBBY: You haven't said anything to the board?

JOHN: This is nothing to do with the board. This is you and me.

BOBBY: *(Beat)* Any beer left? *(JOHN roots in the plastic bag, takes out two cans of beer)*

JOHN: Last two. *(JOHN hands a can to BOBBY. They open the cans)*

BOBBY: *(Beat)* The first one was an accident. *(Beat)* Cheers. *(BOBBY drinks. JOHN follows suit. JOHN puts down his can and suddenly embraces BOBBY fiercely)*

JOHN: *(Emotional)* Jesus! Bobby!

BOBBY: OK. John, OK. It's OK, relax. *(Beat)* You're not on your own anymore. I know what that's like.

JOHN: *(Disengaging)* Is this mental or what?

BOBBY: Everything is, Johnny. Everything is. *(They look at each other a moment)*

JOHN: OK. Business. What have you got?

BOBBY: What way?

JOHN: Gun.

BOBBY: Colt.

JOHN: And that's what? Seven shot?

BOBBY: Yeah.

JOHN: And how accurate?

BOBBY: The gun or me?

JOHN: What's the difference?

BOBBY: Pretty accurate.

JOHN: And how fast?

BOBBY: Full clip?

JOHN: Yeah.

BOBBY: Two...three seconds. Actually probably less. Time sort of stretches out. *(Beat)* The time it takes to count to seven.

JOHN: What?

BOBBY: You count the bullets as you shoot. Helps you concentrate.

JOHN: And the percentage?

BOBBY: Depends.

JOHN: On what?

BOBBY: How many bodies you want. If it's just one guy, you shoot him seven times, last one in the head, he's pretty much dead 100 per cent. Two people, high nineties. Three, they've time to start scattering, percentage drops.

JOHN: If you wanted seven.

BOBBY: One with each bullet?

JOHN: Yeah.

BOBBY: This some sort of economy drive?

JOHN: Seven. What percentage?

BOBBY: Depends how mobile.

JOHN: They're all on a bus going to the Giant's Causeway, remember?

BOBBY: You'd be lucky to get all seven. They start diving. And you can't go too far down the bus, you have to stay by the door to clear off.

JOHN: If you had an Uzi?

BOBBY: *(Beat)* If you had an Uzi, they'd be wallpaper. *(Beat)* They'd dissolve.

JOHN: Double figures?

BOBBY: Oh definitely.

JOHN: *(Considers)* Hmmm.

BOBBY: When were you thinking of?

JOHN: Tomorrow.

BOBBY: Tomorrow?!

JOHN: It's no big plan Bobby. You get on the bus, you shoot everything that moves, you get off the bus — what? Twenty seconds?

BOBBY: *(Beat)* Fifteen.

JOHN: OK. Franklin Hotel, tomorrow morning, ten o'clock, the bus arrives. Bunch of people get on. So do you. Driver thinks you're one of the Swiss, they think you're something to do with the bus. Bang! There you go.

BOBBY: Do I get a driver? Car switch?

JOHN: No. This isn't an operation. No stolen cars, no abandoned cars. This is like we said — comes out of the blue, vanishes into the air. *(Beat)* Can you handle it?

BOBBY: Yes.

JOHN: I know you can. Got your gun?

BOBBY: Yeah.

JOHN: On you?

BOBBY: Why?

JOHN: Because I'm going to get you an Uzi. But you know Billy won't let you have two guns on the go. Gun in gun out, Billy's rules, can't get round them. So you go get your gun and I'll wait here for you.

BOBBY: *(Beat)* I have it here.

JOHN: Great. Give us it. *(JOHN holds his hand out for the gun while consulting his watch)* O.K. so it's...half-one ...two...two-and-a-half...meet here at four. OK? *(Still holding out his hand for the gun, JOHN looks up from his watch at BOBBY)* You want to meet me back here at four? Pick up the Uzi? *(Beat)* Bobby? Two-and-a-half hours? I think you can do without the gun for two-and-a-half hours. You're not Dirty Harry.

BOBBY: *(Beat)* Yeah. OK *(Unbuttons coat, takes gun from a shoulder holster)* Don't like giving it up, you know? *(Hands gun to JOHN)* Sorry.

JOHN: Don't worry about it. Is it loaded?

BOBBY: Of course.

JOHN: *(Nervous)* Shit! Is the safety on?

BOBBY: *(Smiles)* Yeah, don't worry.

JOHN: Ah, right. Good. Ah yeah. Tripoli, eh? *(JOHN hefts the gun in his hand)*

BOBBY: Don't mess with it John, alright?

JOHN: Oh yeah, sure of course. All the same, it has a good...feel to it.

BOBBY: You tell Billy I want that one back, right? And he's not to be handing it out to any young yahoo.

JOHN: Don't worry. I'll get it back to you. *(Beat. JOHN starts singing along to the tape)* All right! Got to turn that up! *(JOHN goes to the radio-cassette, carrying the gun. He turns the music up loud and stands with his back to BOBBY, swaying to the music)*

BOBBY: It's a bit loud.

JOHN: It has to be loud Bobby.

BOBBY: *(Grins, raises beer in a toast)* Ah Johnny, you're a wild man all the same. *(JOHN turns suddenly, clicks off the safety catch and points the gun at BOBBY. Beat)* Come on John, don't mess around. *(Beat)* John, I'm serious! *(Beat)* John! For God's sake!!

JOHN: *(Still pointing gun, walks over to BOBBY, shouting)* One, two, three, four, five, six! *(By now JOHN is next to BOBBY, with the gun pressed to BOBBY's head. They look at each other. Beat)* Seven.

BOBBY: *(Beat)* Put the gun down John.

JOHN: *(Lowers the gun)* Just seeing what it felt like.

BOBBY: *(Beat)* What did it feel like?

JOHN: Too...personal.

BOBBY: (Beat) Only the first one.

JOHN: *(Pockets the gun. Beat)* So I'll see you back here at four?

BOBBY: *(Beat)* Yeah.

JOHN: Good man.

BOBBY: *(Beat)* So. I'll see you, yeah?

JOHN: Yeah.

BOBBY: *(Going)* Alright. Take care. *(BOBBY goes. Beat. JOHN turns off the radio-cassette, removes the tape and puts it in his pocket. He picks up the phone and dials.)*

JOHN: Peter? *(Beat)* Yeah it's me. *(Beat)* You were right. It was Bobby. And he done more than four. There were two others we didn't know about. *(Beat)* Yeah, six poor bastards. *(Beat)* He's coming back here at four. I set it up. Should give you enough time, yeah? *(Beat)* You shouldn't have any trouble. I have his gun. *(Beat)* He gave it to me. *(Beat)* Why? Because we're friends. *(JOHN puts down the phone, surveys the room. Beat. He goes)*

End

FAINT VOICES

A One-Act Play

John MacKenna

For Anne Clarke

Faint Voices, which won the All-Ireland One-Act Festival in 1995, was first produced by the **Prosperous Dramatic Society** on 22nd October 1995 in Prosperous, Co Kildare.

MRS LEDWIDGE	Lurlene Duggan
MATTY MC GOONA	Christy Casey
ELLIE VAUGHEY	Mary McCormack
FRANK LEDWIDGE	John O'Loughlin
NEIGHBOURS	Irene Houlihan
	Mary McCarthy
SOLDIERS	TJ Duggan
	Brian Kehoe

Director	Anne Clarke

INTRODUCTION

Faint Voices is a play based on the love affair between Frank Ledwidge, the Slane poet who was killed in 1917 in the Great War, and Ellie Vaughey, a member of a well-to-do farming family from just outside Slane.

Ledwidge worked at a variety of jobs in and around Slane in the early years of the twentieth century. His poetic talent was encouraged by Lord Dunsany, a local landlord and himself a writer. Ledwidge's promise was cut short by his early death.

The reasons for Ledwidge's joining the British army are complicated. Some people have argued that it was a political decision. Undoubtedly, the loss of Ellie Vaughey's love was a major influence and this factor is the central point of this play.

Ellie Vaughey married a local man and moved to Manchester where she died in childbirth, in June 1915.

FAINT VOICES

I have left the production, set and movement in the hands of the director. The only suggestions I make are that at the opening and closing of the play, Frank and Ellie are framed, as in an old photograph, upstage centre. I don't mean literally framed, rather posed as in a sepia print. At the opening of the play, Mrs Ledwidge and Matty are also on stage—downstage left and right. Beyond this, I suggest the stage be used in areas — Mrs Ledwidge's home, Matty's area, and an orchard area where the lovers meet. But this is merely a suggestion. I would prefer each director to find his/her own approach to the play, as was done in the original production. The other area of differentiation is between the "dead world" of Frank and Ellie and the "living world" of Matty and Mrs Ledwidge. Again, I leave this to the ingenuity of the director.

MRS LEDWIDGE: When I think of him I think of someone still, dead still, lying there pale and still. That's the way I picture him. I know full well it couldn't have been like that. Of course I do. But that's the way I think of him. The way I choose to think of him. For my own peace of mind. I know there's no point tearing myself up inside to think of him in any other way.

MATTY: I think of them more and more. Faced with my own mortality. I think more and more of theirs.

(FRANK & ELLIE giggle.)

ELLIE: *(Gesturing towards audience)* Ssshhh they'll hear us.

FRANK: Not a chance.

ELLIE: They might.

FRANK: Well let them. Feck's sake, Matty, will you don't be getting all high-falutin'.

MRS LEDWIDGE: We were ever a family of soldiers and poets. A great people in this land. All this land once belonged to the Ledwidges. I told him that.

FRANK: Now she's getting as bad.

ELLIE: She's your mother.

FRANK: I know who she is.

ELLIE: *(Indicating audience)* They don't.

FRANK: Well then they must be stupid. Any fool could see that. Mother and son.

MRS LEDWIDGE: I told them all, all the children fanning out from my arms. Paddy, my husband, told it to me, back in the days when we were digging and raking our cottage garden and I sang it to the children, told it to them in bedtime stories, whispered it at night.

ELLIE: Did she?

FRANK: She did.

MRS LEDWIDGE: And the corn mill was ours and the woods as far as Kilcairne. Paddy told me, in the evenings when we sowed the half-acre, told me by firelight, told me at night in bed, when we talked after lovemaking.

FRANK: She goes on about him but when I asked her about my father, her eyes said no, said not to talk of him, and I learned to leave well enough alone.

MRS LEDWIDGE: I think of Paddy, dead. And of Frank dead. And young Ellie Vaughey, dead.

ELLIE: See I told you, she does think of me.

FRANK: The catch I let slip.

MATTY: Mainly, I want to tell you what happened. Them. Us. Frank, Ellie and me.

FRANK: *(Giggling)* He's getting too serious.

ELLIE: He has to.

FRANK: Why?

ELLIE: Because he doesn't know. He knows it all, but in the end, he knows nothing. About now.

FRANK: So?

ELLIE: So let him tell it. Will you?

FRANK: All right. For you.

MATTY: We went back a long way. Frank and me. He said I was a master fiddler. He said I was a mighty footballer, he said the cherries in our orchard were the best in the world. I know he was a bloody fine poet.

MRS LEDWIDGE: There was a clearness in her laughter, young Ellie Vaughey. I could see how much they were in love. She broke his seriousness. Him and Matty could get fierce serious and she'd always have them laughing. I liked to see him laughing. And there was a cleaness about her, light in her face, health in her hair.

ELLIE: See? Now. That's what you missed. And she's right.

FRANK: And the rest of it.

MRS LEDWIDGE: I'd know when he came back from seeing her.

ELLIE: *(Laughing loudly)* Hah! And you thought no one knew.

MATTY: And Ellie Vaughey. I was half in love with her myself. I'd watch her and Frank together, leaning together at a stile or walking the headland of a field or dancing and I'd be jealous.

FRANK: Well, there's something I never knew. He had an eye on you.

ELLIE: And why wouldn't he?

FRANK: But Matty was too serious for that.

ELLIE: Well thanks very much.

MRS LEDWIDGE: I think of him and her. Dead.

(FRANK giggles)

MATTY: For Jesus' sake Frank, stop it!

FRANK: What?

ELLIE: He knows we're here.

MATTY: Stop the bloody cynicism. I hear you.

FRANK: How?

ELLIE: He must be dead.

FRANK: Are you dead?

MATTY: No, I'm not dead. And neither are you, either of you.

ELLIE: Of course we're dead.

MATTY: Not to me. Not yet.

MRS LEDWIDGE: I could go back, but where's the good in it.

FRANK: Can she hear us? *(MATTY shakes his head)* But you can?

MATTY: Yes.

ELLIE: I don't like this.

MATTY: I just knew your voices, knew you were there. Once I started thinking of you. Will you come back here?

ELLIE: Can we?

FRANK: Where are we going back to?

MATTY: I don't know.

FRANK: *(As he speaks, the neighbours come onstage to attend his brother's wake)* Go back to the days when God forgot us. Go back to the days when my brother was dying.

Back to the clots on the pillow, the wrack of his cough in the room, the bailiffs and the police at the door, the way he wasted to nothing, the voices outside while he was dying. Him laid out in the room, the parish burying him, the silence in the morning after he died. If you have to go back, go back to that.

ELLIE: Ssshhh.

FRANK: Hah.

MRS LEDWIDGE & ELLIE & MATTY: (*As they pray, the neighbours leave the stage*) Our Father who art in heaven, hallowed be thy name, thy kingdom come, thy will be done on earth as it is in heaven. Give us this day our daily bread and forgive us our trespasses, as we forgive those who trespass against us and lead us not into temptation but deliver us from evil. Amen.

ELLIE: I want you to kiss me. Kiss me. Don't stand there like a young fool, kiss me. Your tongue makes words for your mouth to say, so kiss me. Tempt me. Whisper words in my ear. Whisper words in my mouth. When I'm working, I think of you. Young and strong and laughing. I make you laugh, your mother says. I take the serious look off your face. Do you remember the Sunday in McGoona's orchard? You and me and Matty watching the bees fall drunk from the cherry trees? I was drunk on you, Frank. You tempted me. Tempt me again, Frank Ledwidge. Sometimes I fancy myself by that name. Ellie Ledwidge. I try it on like a frock. Twirl around a time or two and try it out. I like the sound . Would you?

MRS LEDWIDGE: She was taken by him. Why not? I told her stories about him. When he was working in Lady Conyngham's kitchen, the cook had a slate laid out with the dishes for the lunch and that night's dinner on it. Frank rubbed the slate clean and wrote in 'Pig's feet, cabbage and spuds' and that was the end of him there.

(*ELLIE laughs*)

MRS LEDWIDGE: And then he was off to Dublin, shop keeping. Home in less than a week. Hiding from the postman in Slane in case the word got home before him.

FRANK: I did not.

MRS LEDWIDGE: It was like him and Joe hadn't seen one another for a year.

ELLIE: What age was he then?

MRS LEDWIDGE: Sixteen. And Joe was twelve. You should have seen the light in their eyes, Ellie.

MATTY: You hardly knew him then?

ELLIE: No. But later I knew him well. I'd see him speeding on his bicycle from a football match to home, from the Conyngham Arms to God knows where, always speeding on his bicycle. His face was tanned and his eyes were bright and he always waved when he passed. I wanted him to stop. I went the places he went and hoped to see him there — sometimes I was lucky, sometimes not. He wasn't like some of the others I knew. He was neat and clean. You'd see him of an evening dressed well, washed and fresh after a day at work on the roads. I went to see him in the plays they put on in the hall, him and Joe and all the others from Slane. And then I'd hang around and hope to see him afterwards.

MATTY: And then he went to work in the mine.

MRS LEDWIDGE: The copper mine? Are you mad?

FRANK: The money's good.

MRS LEDWIDGE: Think of the danger.

FRANK: *(Laughing)* There's no danger.

MATTY: Sometimes, in the afternoon, there'd be a rumble and the whole village would go silent, waiting for word to come.

MRS LEDWIDGE: Men were taken out, as pale as death, laid out on boards, pale as death under coppered skin.

ELLIE: Dead men were dragged out like wagons filled with coppered clay.

MATTY: Dead men dragged out and left while the work went on.

FRANK: Dead men, talked about and waked and buried.

MRS LEDWIDGE: And in the evenings, he'd dress and cycle up to see Lord Dunsany. They'd talk about the poems they were writing. He was always on at Frank, encouraging. "Bless us," I'd say, "there's you up there with Lords and look at us down here."

ELLIE: Don't let your head get turned. Don't let your head get turned, don't turn your head away.

MRS LEDWIDGE: But there was only Ellie.

MATTY: (*To ELLIE*) He talked of you.

MRS LEDWIDGE: Always.

MATTY: All the time

FRANK: But not enough. Not enough about the soft pale skin and the laughing face.

ELLIE: Ssshhh. I remember the first night you came to our house.

FRANK: I feel that she will come in blue, with yellow in her hair and two curls strayed out of her comb's loose stocks...

ELLIE: I knew your tricks. Coming late of a Sunday night and asking me to bring your poems to Drogheda for the paper. It took you long enough to notice me, beyond the messenger you made of me.

FRANK: It did.

MATTY: He had his eye on her. But never a word. I'd rise him. You like her, don't you?

(FRANK shrugs)

ELLIE: He liked me but it took him long enough. I'd almost given up hope and then... I was... I was that happy. And the poems he brought were now for me.

FRANK: *I feel that she will come in blue,*
with yellow in her hair
and two curls strayed

> *out of her comb's loose stocks*
> *and I shall steal behind her*
> *and lay my hands upon her eyes*
> *and her peal of laughter will ring far.*
> *And as she tries for freedom*
> *I will call her name to the flowers.*

(ELLIE laughs)

MATTY: You'd hear her laughing. She had a laugh that made you want to laugh with her.

MRS LEDWIDGE: Her laughter was a song

FRANK: Can you not stop laughing?

ELLIE: I can't. I swear to God. I'm sorry. Now read me a poem.

FRANK: *And the blue*
> *of hiding violets, watching for your face,*
> *listen for you in every dusky place.*

ELLIE: *(Laughing loudly)* I'm sorry, Frank...I can't help it. *(She laughs again and then her laughter stops dead)*

MATTY: Sometimes I thought there'd be no end to their happiness.

MRS LEDWIDGE: They made a lovely couple, walking the lane together, him rushing off of a Sunday to see her.

FRANK: There was always a reason.

ELLIE: I knew his knock.

FRANK: She laughed less.

ELLIE: I didn't need to laugh at everything.

FRANK: I was in love but I couldn't find the words.

ELLIE: I knew he was in love with me. My love was as tense as my body, ready to spring, ready to wrap him up inside me. Would that have been so wrong? It would have been the right thing to do. Would have saved our lives. To have him inside of me. Safe. To let our bodies say what our mouths could not. We say it now when it's too late. Too far away.

FRANK: We were in love.

ELLIE: Too late, too far away. Ghosts meeting in a church at night. November night. All saints. All souls. November nights. What about the other nights? Spring nights. Summer. What about the chances come and gone? You buried in your books and me with ...what? Half-remembered chances, half-taken. Whatever I took I took because I needed it. And that was all. Look back whatever way you like, Frank Ledwidge, but I needed more than words.

MATTY: We talked about her, about the way he felt for her. Sometimes she came and sat in our orchard watching the drunken bees fall from the black cherries. She'd laugh.

MRS LEDWIDGE: And then it changed.

MATTY: All changed.

MRS LEDWIDGE: He tried to make light of it.

FRANK: That's the way the world turns.

MATTY: Don't get too serious.

FRANK: You were right

MATTY: Just be careful the way things work out.

MRS LEDWIDGE: I knew, the first Sunday he spent at home in ages.

MATTY: I knew it might happen.

MRS LEDWIDGE: Are you not going up to Ellie's?

FRANK: Not today.

MRS LEDWIDGE: Is anything the matter?

FRANK: No.

MRS LEDWIDGE: Is she not well?

FRANK: She's well.

MRS LEDWIDGE: Are you going out then?

FRANK: I might ride over to Matty's.

ELLIE: Sunday and the ticking clock.

FRANK: I might.

ELLIE: The day dragging on towards darkness.

FRANK: I might

ELLIE: I have to tell you this.

FRANK: Tell me.

ELLIE: I have to.

FRANK: Tell me.

ELLIE: I can't see you again.

FRANK: Can't?

ELLIE: And I was thinking, I love you madman, I love you.

FRANK: Can't?

ELLIE: It's no good, Frank.

FRANK: That's all she said, Matty. Nothing about the acres her family had, nothing about the hard words in the night. Nothing about the things they said of me. The only reason they talked her out of it was because I was a road worker. They with half the Hill of Slane and us with a half-acre garden. And she listened.

MATTY: Maybe because she loved you, Frank.

FRANK: What?

MATTY: Maybe because she saw no hope for you. Maybe you never told her where the hope was.

ELLIE: I might have been stronger but it was too late. What got in the way? Land, family, money, hope or the lack of it. I waited for words, real words, but nothing came. Only verses. Had he no way of saying anything that wasn't in a verse? Had he no way of leaning his head to mine the way he would with

112

others? Did he think I'd always be satisfied with that? He loved me but he never said, never touched me the way I wanted him. And when they sat me down, the family, and pointed out the rest of it, rich and poor, landed and penniless and all that goes with that, I couldn't find a word to say in his defence. All I saw was the gap between us, between what he gave and what I needed and that had nothing to do with money. It had to do with need. Love, touch, kisses, soft words whispered in the dark. Love, touch, kisses. Love, touch, kisses. Love, touch. Love, touch. Love, touch. Touch, touch. Touch me. See, nothing about land or money in that.

MATTY: They told her it wouldn't work and they were right. They knew things better than Ellie or Frank.

FRANK: Tell me.

ELLIE: It just won't work.

FRANK: Is that what your family says?

ELLIE: Just hold my hand, will you?

MATTY: He told me that she put her hand on his shoulder. There was a full moon rising. There was a calmness about her. Her eyes were full of sorrow, he said. Real sorrow.

FRANK: When she folded her arms, I heard wings fluttering.

MATTY: And then he asked her.

FRANK: Is that all?

ELLIE: You never know.

FRANK: Will I hear from you?

ELLIE: Soon. Maybe soon.

MATTY: Her white teeth biting down on her lip.

ELLIE: Maybe.

MATTY: He went in home in the rain, bolted the kitchen door, went into his silent room and lay on the bed. And sleep only wearied him. He told me he dreamed about mortar and bricks and flocks of sheep in rich fields.

ELLIE: I heard the clock chiming all night.

MRS LEDWIDGE: Matty told me, a long time afterwards, that Frank was bent on keeping Ellie. He never gave up hope. Never, as if we can talk of never.

FRANK: Hope is a great thing and I had hope. It was there in everything I did and said and saw. If the sun rose up resplendent there was hope in it. If it sneaked along the shoulder of a field there was hope in that. I drew life from the sun and hope and hope is the greatest thing, the one thing worth talking of. And I had hope. That I could make her change her mind, that we'd find a way round the ditches thrown up in our way, that love would out. I had hope, more hope than I knew what to do with. It set my head singing and my heart racing ahead of me. Oh I had hope.

MATTY: And then word came, the rumour and the gossip, that Ellie was walking out with John O'Neill. A handsome man. Did you hear that Ellie is seeing John O'Neill?

MRS LEDWIDGE: Does Frank know yet?

(MATTY shakes his head)

MRS LEDWIDGE: Someone should tell him, before he meets them on the road.

MATTY: Will I tell him?

MRS LEDWIDGE: Do.

MATTY: And I did. John O'Neill who plays the fiddle, dances, sings. He knows there's more to love than words.

ELLIE: What was I to do Matty? Tied in on every side by my family and Frank's coldness. John was a handsome man. Dapper. He'd lift me round the dance floor, my feet off the ground. Head spinning, heart racing, eyes closed, kisses in my hair. Telling me how beautiful... how beautiful.

FRANK: I tried to lose myself in other eyes but nothing came of it. And then the war.

MRS LEDWIDGE: And then the war.

MATTY: The people who knew him least thought he joined for high ideals. He joined because the British army stood between us and the enemy of our civilisation and he wouldn't have it said that we were defended while we did nothing. But there was another reason.

FRANK: What else is there to do? Everywhere I go, their shadows fall in front of me.

ELLIE: I heard the stories. Snipes in the street at John and me. Slane is a small place.

MRS LEDWIDGE: And the letters came, saying all was well. Saying he missed the Conyngham Arms. Words about summer nights in Slane.

FRANK: But I was drifting far away.

ELLIE: And I had no way of knowing.

FRANK: I always keep remembering the little things.

ELLIE: There are things I can't forget.

MATTY: And then he saw it. In the paper that I sent him.

FRANK: *(Reading)* O'Neill and Vaughey in St Patrick's RC church, Slane. By the Rev F Fagan, CC, Slane. John O'Neill (Rossin) to Ellen Mary (Ellie), only daughter of the late John and Mrs Vaughey, Hill of Slane, Co Meath.

MATTY: What did he expect?

ELLIE: What did you expect?

FRANK: I expected to go back to you when this war was straightened out.

MRS LEDWIDGE: He came home for Christmas but he was changed. The spark was gone out of him. And all the coaxing wouldn't bring it back. The same week that he was home, young Jack Tiernan, a neighbour's child, was killed. There was nothing left of that black year. He left verses written of the boy:

He will not come and still I wait,
he whistles at another gate
where angels listen. Ah, I know
he will not come, yet if I go
how shall I know he did not pass
barefooted in the flowery grass.

MATTY: *The moon leans on one silver horn*
above the silhouettes of morn
and, from their nest sills, finches whistle
or stooping pluck the downy thistle.

ELLIE: *How is the morn so gay and fair*
without his whistling in the air?
The world is calling, I must go.

FRANK: *How shall I know he did not pass,*
barefooted in the shining grass?

ELLIE: How was I to know?

FRANK: I miss the bog in Wilkinstown. When you hear the blackbird singing, think of me.

ELLIE: I do.

FRANK: I remember the crows flying from Wilkinstown to Slane. I see all the old landmarks as I cross the fields in my dreams.

ELLIE: And so do I. From this single room in Manchester.

MATTY: Him gone back to the war. Her gone with John O'Neill to Manchester. Go where the work is, I heard him say. But her step was less light there.

FRANK: They'll be planting spuds in Carlonstown now and I'm back, in my head, in the kitchens around Slane.

ELLIE: And so am I. Far away from the black streets of Manchester.

MRS LEDWIDGE: We heard the news from her family. But Frank told me he had a dream that night.

FRANK: There were white birds flying above the sea and I was on the ground, watching them. The dream haunted me. I knew there was something wrong. Some feeling that there was something wrong.

MRS LEDWIDGE: She died.

MATTY: In the back streets of Manchester.

MRS LEDWIDGE: It all went wrong.

ELLIE: Unhappy in my marriage. Away from Slane. Pregnant. Sick. I wasn't made for housekeeping. I couldn't keep a house. I fell out of love. Unhappy, sick, the colour gone from my face, my teeth decayed, my daughter born as I was dying.

FRANK: I went to see her laid out in a room in Manchester but it wasn't her. It was someone else. She was gone, escaped.

MATTY: He wrote her a poem.

FRANK: *A blackbird singing on a moss upholstered stone,*
bluebells swinging, shadows wildly blown,
a song in the wood, a ship on the sea,
the song was for you and the sorrow for me.

ELLIE: He wrote me a poem.

MATTY: *A blackbird singing I hear in my troubled mind,*
bluebells swinging I see in a distant wind,
but sorrow and silence are the wood's threnody,
the silence for you and the sorrow for me.

MRS LEDWIDGE: Gallipoli. The smell of dead corpses.

FRANK: Stuck in a ditch for hours. Pinned down by gunfire. Remembering Slane. Did that cow with the timber tongue survive or die?

MRS LEDWIDGE: Egypt, England. Sickness, health.

ELLIE: He came back home with me. Did you know that?

MATTY: No.

ELLIE: He did. He came back home. With me. Followed my spirit from Manchester.

MRS LEDWIDGE: Dublin in flames and Frank back here, back home in Slane.

ELLIE: He came back looking for me, under every bush, on the headland of every field, at every stile. Expecting me on every street.

MRS LEDWIDGE: Picquigny. Winter at the front. And spring. And summer once again.

MATTY: He spent his birthday in a little red town in France. In an orchard.

ELLIE: Thinking of me.

FRANK: There's a lovely valley below me and a river that goes gobbling down the fields like turkeys coming home in Ireland. It's an idle little vagrant that does no work for miles and miles.

ELLIE: He sleeps out in the orchard and every morning the cuckoo comes to a tree nearby and calls his name.

FRANK: I think of Slane Hill. Blue and distant.

ELLIE: And of me there. With a blue ribbon in my hair.

FRANK: Can you hear me Matty?

MATTY: What?

FRANK: Can you hear me?

MATTY: I hear you.

FRANK: It must be beautiful out on the bog now.

MATTY: It is.

FRANK: How happy to be living in peace. Out here the land is broken up with shells and the woods are like skeletons.

(MATTY nods)

FRANK: But once I heard a bird singing in all of this and I stopped and listened.

ELLIE: And his heart lifted with hope.

FRANK: Hope.

ELLIE: Hope. Hope. Hope. There's hope for us Frank. My heart is lifting yours, lifting with you.

FRANK: (*As he speaks, the other soldiers in his group appear as a tableau behind him*) A terrible rainstorm sweeping over us. The place is grey. Land and sky. We stop our work and sit in the half-shelter, drinking tea.

ELLIE: He thinks of me.

FRANK: I do. And I try to remember the bird singing and the other birds in Slane. And you laughing. But I can hear nothing. Only the rain rattling on my tin mug. The rain on my helmet. The rain on my sodden boots. The rain on my coat. I watch the rain slide down the handle of the shovel I'm holding.

ELLIE: Ssshhh.

MATTY: It was the last day of July.

ELLIE: He knows.

MATTY: (*Indicating audience*) They don't

(*ELLIE nods*)

MATTY: It was the last day of July. He was on a digging party, resting between trench digs.

MRS LEDWIDGE: (*Reading*) "Dear Mrs Ledwidge, I don't know how to write to you about the death of your son Francis. We had many talks together and he used to read me his poems. He died on the feast of St Ignatius Loyola. The evening before he died, he had been to Confession. On the morning of the thirty-first, he was present at Mass and received Holy Communion. That evening, whilst out with a working party, a shell exploded quite near them, killing seven and wounding twelve. Francis was killed at once so he suffered no pain. I like to think God took him before the world would be able to spoil him with its praise and he has found greater joy and beauty than he would have found on earth." (*During this reading, the soldiers, apart from Frank, have disappeared*)

FRANK: Is that what it said?

MATTY: She needed it.

FRANK: What about me, what did I need?

ELLIE: Frank!

FRANK: All right, all right, but why are we here?

MATTY: I knew if one came you'd both come.

FRANK: And...?

MATTY: The night you died, I was locking up in the print works. It was after two in the morning. When I was turning, I could've sworn I saw you on the far side of the street. I called you. I thought you were home on leave.

ELLIE: He was looking for me.

FRANK: I heard you. But there wasn't time Matty, I was in a hurry. I had to find her, I knew she'd be here somewhere.

ELLIE: I was waiting.

MATTY: I knew it. There were times I'd be sitting at home, winter nights at the fire, or long evenings pulling on for dusk in the orchard and I'd... I'd... know they were there. The pair of them. I didn't dare tell anyone. I sensed they were there. I never gave up hope. I often told the pair of them not to give up hope, when they were drifting apart. I loved the pair of them. All I could do was tell the pair of them never to give up hope. Sometimes I nearly gave up hope myself and then I'd remember things. Frank, flying along on his bike, gabbling that fast I could hardly keep up with him. Or Ellie laughing. I never forgot that laugh. The sweetest. I never forgot either of them, not for a minute.

End